'*Burnt Eucalyptus W[...]* at once a love story [...] anthem. It is compuls[...] while remaining uncompromising in its assessments and realisations. Take note: this astonishing book announces the arrival of a rare voice, wise beyond her years. Perhaps beyond all of ours.'

Maaza Mengiste, author of *The Shadow King*

'In the midst of so much pessimism, especially among young people, this book is like a crack of light in the dark. […] Compulsory reading.'

Time Out

'The author mixes the sentimental, intimate and evoc-ative, which she knows first-hand, with statistics and reports on the African social and economic reality, which she has in turn handled in her occupations in various international organizations in Nairobi, Brussels and Maastrich. […] The narrator evokes the scenarios, routes, places, colours and smells of her childhood, with-out avoiding the harshest episodes but in such a way that the pleasant feelings from the country where she lived until she was seven years old carry more weight overall.'

La Vanguardia

THE
INDIGO
PRESS

BURNT
EUCALYPTUS
WOOD

BURNT EUCALYPTUS WOOD

On Origins, Language and Identity

ENNATU DOMINGO

THE
INDIGO
PRESS

THE INDIGO PRESS
50 Albemarle Street
London W1S 4BD
www.theindigopress.com

The Indigo Press Publishing Limited Reg. No. 10995574
Registered Office: Wellesley House, Duke of Wellington Avenue
Royal Arsenal, London SE18 6SS

First published in Great Britain in 2023 by The Indigo Press

First published in Catalan in 2022 as *Fusta
d'eucaliptus cremada* by Navona Editorial

A CIP catalogue record for this book is available from the British Library

ISBN: 978-1-91164-858-1
eBook ISBN: 978-1-91164-860-4

Translation of 'Divisa' by Maria-Mercè Marçal
(*Cau de Llunes*, 1977) © Sam Abrams

Front cover painting by Bekelech Tamayo
Cover design by Luke Bird
Art direction by House of Thought
Printed and bound in Great Britain by TJ Books Limited, Padstow
Typeset in Goudy Old Style by Tetragon, London

CONTENTS

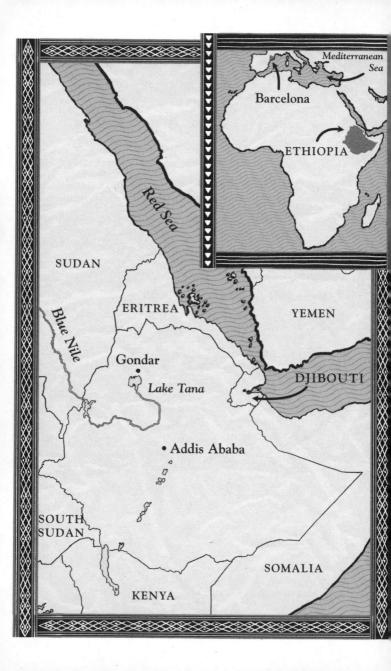

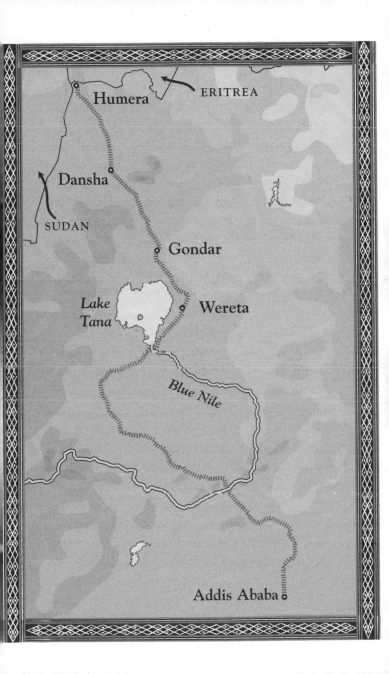

BESIDE THE WINDOW

We left Dansha for Wereta in a hot, jam-packed bus filled with a sharp smell of sweat. The air was dense and it was difficult to breathe. The parched road was narrow, and every time we met another vehicle it seemed as though we might come off it altogether. There were many potholes and the driver had to brake constantly to avoid them if he didn't want the bus to overturn. I was sitting beside the window with my little brother on my lap, I was seven and he was three, but he weighed hardly anything. Mikaele had a high fever and was so weak he no longer even cried. Even had he done so, out of thirst or hunger, I had nothing to give him. We'd already finished the *dabo** and there was no water left. We weren't carrying any luggage, just a few birr. We wore everything we had.

Through the dirty window I could see the flat landscape we were leaving behind. It was still the dry

---

* The definitions of words in Amharic can be found in the glossary at the end of the book.

season, but we were entering the greenest, wettest, most mountainous part of Ethiopia. From time to time we would overtake a horse-drawn carriage, a group of women carrying bundles of vegetables on their heads or umbrellas, to shield themselves from the sun, walking along the side of the road. The bumps made my forehead pound against the glass.

Suddenly, out of the corner of my eye, I glimpsed a teacher from the school in Dansha among the bus passengers. I'd only gone to school for one day, one day in my whole life, and he probably wouldn't recognise me, but, just in case, I covered my face with my white cotton *netela* and hugged Mikaele tightly to my chest. I didn't want him to ask how my mother was. Wasn't it clear she was very unwell? Sitting beside me, Yamrot had vomited into the aisle of the bus minutes earlier, and the people around us looked at us in disgust. She was coughing a lot and her *netela* was bloodstained. No one offered to help us. By then their aid wouldn't have been much use: Yamrot's state seemed irreversible.

The bus was going to Gondar. I knew it took two days to go from Dansha to Wereta, and Gondar was the halfway point. Perhaps we would have to spend the night at the bus stop, as we had done before, and wait for the next bus.

What I didn't know was that this dusty road would bring me to a horizon beyond anything I could imagine.

A NEW WAR IN
THE NORTH

On 4 November 2020 I woke up in the early hours of the morning in a small, welcoming flat in the centre of Brussels. Outside it was still night and the streets of the city were empty and silent. The windows were misted up. I reached out from under the duvet to grab my mobile from the bedside table. I opened Twitter almost without thinking.

'The prime minister of Ethiopia, Abiy Ahmed, has ordered a military intervention in Tigray,' I read, in a tweet by a local journalist that was going viral. The whole world was focused on the US election, in which Joe Biden and Donald Trump were contesting the presidency for the next four years. And Tigray, one of the ten states of the Ethiopian federation, had gone offline. Blacked out, with no access to information. I wouldn't get back to sleep now. I knew that within a few hours that tweet would blow up on international media. My muscles tensed; I was aware that, like most people, I would be able to do nothing more than watch the number of deaths climb. The information that came trickling through drop by drop would be manipulated by both sides of the conflict in an attempt to exert control over the official narrative, causing us to lose the thread of events. And in the end there would be silence, leaving space for anxious reflection, paving the way for the next wave of violence. It was as if a bucket of water was full of holes and we lacked hands to cover them. A pattern of behaviour which had become endemic in the country, difficult to break.

The central Ethiopian government was saying that the TPLF (Tigray People's Liberation Front) had attacked the military base in Humera, one of the best-fortified with soldiers, artillery and equipment. The reason this military base was so important was its proximity to Eritrea, which until very recently had represented the greatest threat to Ethiopian security. Even though the war with Eritrea had ended in 2001, having started in 1998, the military base was equipped in case of attacks on the border and was therefore still active. An attack on the Ethiopian military base meant an attack on Ethiopia and its unity.

But had it actually been a preventive attack by the TPLF? It had been clear for months that the central Ethiopian government wanted to remove the government of Tigray, which is where the elite that had ruled Ethiopia for three decades came from and which was resisting changes resulting from the political shift that had brought Abiy Ahmed's administration to power. What's more, a few days before the attack on the military base, Ethiopian soldiers had been seen approaching the Tigray border. Soon after, the federal government took back military control of Dansha, Humera and Mekelle – the capital of Tigray – but, fighting alongside Eritrean soldiers, it continued a guerrilla war against TPLF members.

At twenty-four years old, I was more than five thousand kilometres away from Ethiopia. The towns of my childhood were being bombed and I'd never felt so confused about my roots. Nor so disappointed, and naive for believing that the road to Ethiopian political stability – the key to its development – would be easy. It seemed the federal government and the government of Tigray had come to the conclusion that, to construct the democratic and prosperous Ethiopia they wanted, and that the people demanded, they had to self-destruct in a battle for political hegemony.

It was the first time I'd seen Dansha and Humera become international news. My stomach churned – a feeling I'd learned to recognise, because it forced me to redefine my identity; it pulled me back to my roots. It forced me to recover those images of the streets of Dansha and Humera which my head had erased so long ago. I've heard it said that only pain can reconnect you to buried memories, and I'd rationalised my pain to such an extent that an image of a woman carrying a half-asleep little boy on her back failed to move me. But this image, which had been exploited by opportunistic Western photographers, was also an image etched inside me, an echo of my past. At that moment, I felt a lump in my throat and my eyes filled with tears. My vision became blurry. I couldn't continue reading and I switched to another article.

υ

In July 2003, at seven years old, in the Ethiopian capital Addis Ababa, I explained to my new parents Anna and Ricard that I'd lived in Dansha and Humera. Their Ethiopian friends Kumbi and Teddy were interpreting for us. As the orphan children of soldiers who had been sent to Cuba to study during the 1970s in a kind of exchange programme between communist countries devised by Fidel Castro, they spoke impeccable Spanish with Cuban accents. When they suggested that perhaps I'd come from Welkait (an administrative area of the Amhara region annexed by Tigray during the leadership of TPLF and recovered by Amhara soldiers during the war in 2020), I repeated that I'd worked in the cotton fields between Dansha and Humera with my mother, Yamrot.

During the snatches of free time between the different bureaucratic procedures Anna and Ricard had to undergo to adopt me legally, we crisscrossed the city looking for a decent map on which we might locate my home towns. I didn't know what a map was then. I didn't know how to read or write. It was so difficult to find a map showing the two place names, Dansha and Humera. It was as though they didn't exist. I insisted that these were my home towns: I had never been so clear about who I was and where I came from.

At the Ethiopian Mapping Authority they requested a letter from us explaining why we wanted a map. It had been barely three years since the open war with Eritrea had ended. The military bases were still active because all the Algiers Agreement of 2000 had resulted in was the cessation of hostilities between the two factions – the Eritrean faction then led by Isaias Afewerki and the Ethiopian faction headed by Meles Zenawi – as they negotiated the border between the new independent Eritrean state and Ethiopia. In particular they were fighting over a town named Badimme, which had been assigned to Eritrea by the Ethiopian-Eritrean Boundary Commission but which, according to the Ethiopians, belonged under their jurisdiction, even though Eritrea had used it as a strategic enclave to control the border. Later on, the loss of Eritrea and access to the Red Sea would be significant setbacks for Ethiopia given that, as a landlocked country, it would have to depend on neighbouring ports to access the global market.

I left Ethiopia with an official map in my backpack on which I'd marked the most significant places of my short life there. From the south working northwards, I circled Wereta (where I'd always been told I was born), Gondar, Dansha and Humera: a westward line, between the Ethiopian borders with Eritrea and with Sudan. At seven I said goodbye to everything I knew. Looking out of the window of the Ethiopian Airlines plane at the sprawling city of Addis Ababa as it gradually grew smaller, I was moving away from the landscapes of my life with the feeling that nothing was left for me there and I'd never come back.

Λ

I did go back to Dansha again with Anna and Ricard in 2006, three years after I'd left. I was ten and couldn't remember my street or the house in which I'd lived. That memory can be so blocked has always made me think about the fragility of the human mind. Who would I be without the complexity of my identity? I probably wouldn't see the world as I do, nor have the ambitions I do; I'd probably be calmer, and misery and failure wouldn't scare me so much.

My parents insisted we go to the city of Humera to visit all the places of my nomadic childhood. We arrived after travelling many kilometres on complicated roads from Addis Ababa. We were emotionally and physically exhausted. A sense of calm overcame me, knowing we could travel no further, because Ethiopia ended at Humera so we were forced to stop there.

That was my first time in Humera. I'd never entered the city with Yamrot, as we had remained on the outskirts, living and working in the cotton fields. I don't remember how long we spent there. Probably not as long as I imagine. So I didn't remember Humera, a name that has become an iconic place in my story, a point of reference, like a lighthouse. I was ten and confronting my past for the first time, I was grieving, recovering feelings and images. It was then that I discovered that Humera was a border city between Ethiopia and Eritrea, and how different it was from the Amhara region, where many people had recognised me as one of them. At night, incense was burned in houses and the air had a seductive and earthy fragrance that wrapped around everything.

We walked through the market looking at the stalls heaped with oranges, bananas hanging from a line and kitchen utensils handmade from wood, brass, recycled tins and vegetable fibres of all kinds. We were always with Kumbi, who accompanied us for the whole trip as our interpreter, and Derriba, the driver of our jeep. I doubt we'd have gone there if we'd been aware of the instability of the area. In fact, we ended up sleeping at the United Nations base, with our jeep parked beside the white tanks and other armoured vehicles used by the Blue Helmets.

One afternoon we sat down outside a small *bunna bet* in the street, and Kumbi, Ricard and I began playing chequers, with a board made of cardboard and counters that were nothing other than Mirinda and Pepsi bottle tops. I was calm because I was in a place where no one recognised me and which I didn't have to recognise. Neither the city nor its people claimed me, nor I them. I was still in shock at having lost my main communication tool, Amharic. I felt fake. A traitor. I was Ethiopian but maybe I wasn't any more; I was trying to be an Ethiopian but maybe I didn't look like one any longer.

ሐ

When I began to see that having spent more years in Catalonia than I'd been able to live in my country of origin meant my Catalan and European cultures were increasingly imposing themselves on my Ethiopian and African identity, the subject of human development began to interest me more. It was difficult for me to accept the discourse of victimhood, which meant explaining my experience according to the narrative of guilt, individuality and gratitude. A discourse that made me feel very small. Guilt, because many societies which provide humanitarian aid have no real intention of rectifying structural inequality. They only practise charity to satisfy their conscience, in an attempt to balance a system of structural inequality from which they benefit. Individuality, because I restricted myself to trying to understand why I was the one living outside Ethiopia, and not some other girl from Kombolcha, Desi or the streets of Addis Ababa. It seemed to me that the correct question was: why us and why still? And gratitude, a discourse that obliged you to be thankful for having left, for having been saved from a 'barbarous, poor and ignorant' world. A discourse that left you trapped in the role of victim.

Reality, however, is always more complex. I felt I'd been uprooted and 'transplanted' into a society where it was almost impossible for me to find role models. For that reason I've always resisted people's expectations of me. The wilder and moodier I was, the more connected I felt to that little girl from the mountains of Wereta I still carried within me. Perhaps without meaning to, I began a silent resistance. A resistance to forgetting that at times would also become a fight against myself and against the new world I now inhabited.

THE LUXURY
OF SILENCE

In 2020, the Covid lockdown measures resulted in the breach of the global supply chain and the temporary loss of millions of jobs. It had a huge impact on young people starting their professional lives. It also affected those who depended on casual work and those whose income only allowed them to live day-to-day. How many fathers and mothers were there in Ethiopia who felt they couldn't offer any future to their teenage sons and daughters? For just fifty euros a month I could help pay for a good education in a school in Addis Ababa for the daughter of friends, with all books and materials included. The situation of my friends' daughter was a reminder that although my surroundings had changed, precariousness persisted for most, and was still the everyday reality for those left behind by people like me.

Like many other young people in Catalonia, I'd left home thinking I was doing so forever. After I was repatriated from Kenya, where I'd found my first job, going back to being locked down in my parents' house was like going back to square one. And I didn't know how long I'd have to wait before the rhythm of the world returned to normal – if it ever did.

At the beginning of October 2020, I'd been awarded a Schuman traineeship to work in what would be my second job at the European Parliament in Brussels, in the Department of External Affairs, in the field of the European Union's relations with the countries of Africa, the Caribbean and the Pacific. It seemed to me a privilege to be part of that institution at an important, watershed moment.

The legal framework for relations between Europe and seventy-nine African, Caribbean and Pacific countries was the Cotonou Agreement, ratified in 2000, which replaced the Lomé Convention of 1975. That legal framework was coming to an end and the heads of state had begun negotiations to update and redefine it. The actions of the European Union were under scrutiny in Africa, because the EU was perceived as a prisoner of its own historic bid to promote its values and political ideology. At a time of political affirmation for the African continent, many of us saw that Europe wasn't adapting to the new rhythm of Africa. In fact, over recent years, the European Union had experienced a crisis of purpose aggravated by Brexit and the rise of politically conservative and anti-democratic ideologies in Poland, Hungary and Spain. The confluence of these social and political phenomena exposed an institution that risked being left behind and losing its credibility when it came to projecting its values beyond its borders. It needed to see Africa as a continent with great potential on a global scale. Governments around the world were trying to extract wealth from the African continent, where 60 per cent of the population is under thirty years old. In the long run the European Union was gambling with its relevance to the African continent, especially if the latter managed to take advantage of the resources it obtained from other emerging geopolitical actors.

∞

In the months that followed that first tweet in the early hours of 4 November 2020, Dansha and Humera were headline news in the international press, while institutions such as the European Union tried unsuccessfully to send a message to Abiy Ahmed to stop an 'unnecessary' war. Within days, the conflict had forced the displacement of more than fifty thousand people, who now sought refuge in Sudan, of whom twelve thousand were boys and girls, many unaccompanied. It was distressing to think that choosing violence to resolve this or any conflict meant destroying the futures of so many children. Turkey, the United Arab Emirates and Russia were selling weapons to the Ethiopian government, while, on the other side, the guerrillas were mobilising underage boys, contrary to the UN Convention on the Rights of the Child.

What future does a society have if it deprives the next generation of opportunities and, above all, of a family and the stability required in the early years of life? Violence feeds on misery. We must be more vigilant about the impact of political decisions on people's lives. Weapons must not be sold to governments when we can trace their use against innocent civilians. We must stop normalising the abject misery of almost half the world's population for the benefit of the minority who enjoy a high standard of living.

Going from one tweet to another on Twitter I'd learned that every historical fact can be used for opposing purposes. People who comment on tweets from the camouflage of anonymous names are perfect examples for social analysis, especially when a piece of fake news is amplified at vertiginous speed in an unregulated space. Disinformation is the political tool of my generation, a distinguishing tool in the geopolitical race. The arrival of the internet at the end of the twentieth century has been a revelation, an instrument of globalisation, and direct access to information from remote places has changed the lives of many, but even today the vast majority of the world's population doesn't have access to it. And that is a problem, in an era in which globalisation takes a new form. The African continent continues to be the territory in which economic powers carry out campaigns of disinformation most frequently. And that costs us dearly.

As a young person beginning to form my own ideas, I was shaken by this manipulative evil on the internet; it attuned me to the incendiary effect of words formulated at the opportune moment and in the hands of people intent on destabilisation. Looking at Ethiopia through my screen has taught me that the line separating freedom of speech and the control of information for political uses is very fine. In 2020 in Ethiopia, a country of more than one hundred and twenty million inhabitants, there were only six million social media users and only around twenty-one million had access to the internet. This imbalance greatly impacted how information was disseminated and how it was interpreted away from the digital world. Most importantly, this low level of connectivity has had a direct impact on the economic output of the country and the region of East Africa.

What is to be done when a state not only fails in its responsibility to offer services equitably but also fails to impose order and guarantee the physical safety of its citizens? What is to be done when a government does not condemn violence and focuses instead on defining an abstract enemy that supposedly sabotages the country's progress towards gaining legitimacy by means of military coercion? But above all, how can a 'transition' to a democracy be possible when the government plans to reform itself using tactics from its repressive past? How can it break that vicious circle of violence when its people want to exploit the potential of their country?

Over the years I became less interested in questions about my personal experience and the fate of the seven-year-old girl from Gondar. I was convinced that structural questions would help me get answers about the economic and educational development of people in rural Ethiopia, of women like my mother, Yamrot, and of girls like the one I had been. According to the World Bank, in 2019, 80 per cent of the Ethiopian population lived in rural areas, and this group contained the poorest citizens of the country.

w

The prime minister, Abiy Ahmed, was awarded the Nobel Prize for Peace in 2019. According to the Prize Committee, based in Oslo, he was chosen 'for his efforts to achieve peace and international cooperation, and in particular for his decisive initiative to resolve the border conflict with neighbouring Eritrea'. It is true that a peace treaty signed in Saudi Arabia in 2018 put an end to almost two decades of military impasse with Eritrea over the border conflict, and allowed economic and diplomatic relations to be reinstated between the two countries. As well as being a peacemaker in the region, Abiy Ahmed represented the possibility of significant political and economic reform for the country. A shift towards the capitalist, liberal model that, according to Western powers, needed to be rewarded.

In 2018, Ethiopia's average annual growth was 9.9 per cent, double the annual average of most African countries, which was only 4 per cent of GDP. But the benefits of economic growth still hadn't improved the standard of living for many rural Ethiopian families. Even though the poverty index had been significantly reduced, less than half the population had access to electricity, drinking water and sanitation. The country had made important progress over the past twenty years, but there was still much to be done.

In 2020 in Tigray, almost half the population lived under threat of famine. A UN study warned that, eight months after the beginning of the war, 350,000 people were suffering from hunger. The figures would continue to rise if there was not an immediate response to the perennial humanitarian crisis in the region. International institutions pressed for a ceasefire, which Abiy Ahmed's government ended up declaring unilaterally, for a short while in mid-2021, to allow farmers to plough the land and make up for lost time.

War fractures the social order, destroys infrastructure and alters people's lives forever. The idea that everything I knew could disappear or be transformed made me dizzy. I'd wanted for a while to go back to

Dansha again, haunted by a growing conviction that I wouldn't be able to move forward if I didn't gather up all the different threads of my past in Ethiopia. Seeing Dansha and Humera marked on maps used to illustrate the movements of the military forces into Tigray sharpened my obsession with understanding myself, with not being detached from memories, with knowing where my individual experience fit in to those twenty years of political history.

This became clearer still to me on reading this fragment from *Tierra de mujeres* (*Land of Women*) by María Sánchez:

'Silence is a luxury that we can't allow ourselves,' wrote Chimamanda Ngozi Adichie. And I couldn't agree more. Even if we doubt, even if we feel insecure. Even if we're afraid. We must speak, raise our voices, write. The rural world and its women don't need a literature to save them, but they do need one that tells the truth about them. One that's honest and sincere, that truly gives space to its characters. That doesn't look over shoulders, that doesn't judge or demand, that lets them make mistakes, as we all do, that finally explains and writes their story. Because we cannot remain silent.

I couldn't remain silent any more.

UNDER THE SHADE
OF THE *WARKA*

Yamrot was my mother, but her story doesn't belong to me. I like to think it's a reflection of the story of millions of women in rural Ethiopia. They play an important role in the country's agriculture, which is the main driver of the Ethiopian economy. But despite their contribution to society, they still don't benefit from institutions that incorporate gender policies into their development programmes, no matter how much priorities began to change after Abiy Ahmed's arrival.

Western feminism has begun to take root in Addis Ababa, Bahir Dar and Mekelle, but these are places which remain far from the reality of countrywomen. We're talking about an urban feminism that still marginalises the contributions and needs of rural women. It's a feminism that misunderstands them: many campaigners have taken away their decision-making ability, others have turned them into representatives of an idyllic, folkloric world. An illiterate world immersed in abject poverty. Clearly, as in all rural worlds, there are those who live on the margins of these descriptions. But I will speak only of my experience, of that rural world that shaped the early years of my childhood. When I speak of the women of rural Ethiopia, I'm speaking above all of the women from families that sell agricultural products in local markets; of the women who work fields that are not theirs; of the temporary workers who work in cotton fields or cook *injera* in a cafe-restaurant or sell *arake*. One way or another, Yamrot did all these things.

Yamrot was born at the end of the 1970s in Debre Tabor, a town situated on the road that links Bahir Dar and Gondar, the two big cities of the state of Amhara. Like so many girls in rural Ethiopia, she was married off very young, to Alamnew, a peasant who lived in the mountains of Wereta, a town to the east of Lake Tana, south of Gondar. She was only eighteen when I was born in a *gojo*, in a little village where there must have been scarcely five other adobe houses with roofs of wood and straw, and where a very tall and majestic *warka* stood, a hundred-year-old tree that had resisted the massive plantations of eucalyptus, which grew faster and gave more wood. The smell of burnt eucalyptus wood permeated everything. Not long before, Yamrot had had my brother Getachew, with whom I spent the best moments of my early childhood there, grazing the family's and neighbours' cows on the green and infinite surrounding fields, going to fetch water in the well, both of us mounted on a mule with plastic cans tied on tightly like saddlebags, always having something to recount in the evenings in front of the fire. We'd stretch out on the grass, facing the blue sky and a blazing sun that seemed immense to us. We imagined we'd stay in that position forever, blinking, playing with the sun's rays, arms crossed behind our heads, legs spread. We lived in a valley ringed by mountains, surrounded by yellow flowers called *adey abeba*. It was a place untouched by the outside world, almost two thousand metres above sea level.

Yamrot's third child died just after birth. No one in the family was able to empathise with her loss and depression. They didn't understand why there was so much fuss. Women like her who give birth at home and in remote places put both the baby's and their own lives at risk. Physical strength alone isn't enough in a place where medical facilities are non-existent. The hardship of living in the countryside had taught everyone not to hold out hope for a baby until it could walk and fend for itself. Until then there was the risk that little ones could stray too far from home and get lost; or simply fall down when unsupervised and hit their head so badly they were left as invalids or with long-term disabilities. Losing a child and dying in childbirth were tragic events that were part of daily life. I've always heard it said that parents named their child only once they were sure it would live. All four of us – my older brother Getachew, my younger brother Mikaele, the little one who died before even being named and I – were born at home.

Neighbours in the *gojo*, mothers and daughters, women and girls of all ages, we would walk to the nearest stream to get water in plastic cans, or climb a hill to collect firewood. And we'd tie it to our backs with string to carry it back.

2

Even though water has been declared a basic right, in 2021 only one in every three people worldwide had access to drinking water, so the UN's Sustainable Development Goals were essential for creating a society in which natural resources were fairly distributed, especially in areas under increased climate and demographic pressure, as was happening in Africa (despite it being the continent that produces only 1.3 per cent of global carbon dioxide emissions). In Ethiopia, as in so many other places on the planet, there is plenty of water, but it cannot be collected and used for domestic or agricultural use. During the rainy season, life can be brutal: where the infrastructure is fragile, connections break, there is no transport of any kind, entire towns can be left without electricity, and the cooking firewood remains wet in the areas electricity has never reached.

ñ

I liked watching Yamrot and the neighbouring women dry the *berbere* mixture of spices with garlic, putting it out in the sun on a sheet of plastic weighted down by four stones so the wind wouldn't carry it off. From time to time they would stir it with some long sticks to ensure it was drying. The scent was smoky and hot. When it was completely dry, they'd throw handfuls of the spice and garlic mixture into a big wooden mortar and two women would take turns to grind it: first one would grind, then the other. When they took a break to wipe away the sweat, there were moments of conversation, short exchanges during which they caught up on the goings-on of the neighbourhood. They'd talk about everything. About some family member or friend who had gone abroad to seek work; or about young girls who had left the protection and monotony of the town to go and work in the cities, which had become areas of development and a political point of reference; about those who had left on top of a lorry or inside a bus and who no one had ever seen again; or about women who left their children behind to go and work in countries with more inclusive and progressive laws, such as Uganda, or on the other side of the Red Sea, sending money from Saudi Arabia or Yemen… Some were perhaps able to get hold of documents so they could leave on an aeroplane, but others travelled through Eritrea or Djibouti and faced the consequences. Few received the news about the trafficking of women and children, and would keep asking what had happened to them, I imagine.

ሸ

In 2021, as governmental transparency improved, a misappropriation of public funds came to light: a scandal of misspent money, which had been supposed to be used to track Ethiopian domestic workers trapped in Saudi Arabia with no passports, no means of communicating with their loved ones, no wages, abused and raped by the men of the families for whom they worked. Desperate, many would throw themselves from windows as the ultimate escape from a racist, sexist and enslaving system.

ቀ

Yamrot and her neighbours would move the sheet of plastic to follow the rays of the sun, they would pound the wooden mortar with unhurried blows, they would talk and talk until they had ground the last granule of spice.

Alamnew was becoming increasingly aggressive and impatient about Yamrot's lack of desire to live after losing her third child. One evening, while Yamrot, my brother Getachew and I were in front of the fire made from a few eucalyptus logs, where the pot of *genfo* – a purée made from flour, butter and milk – was cooking, he arrived home drunk after too much *arake* with other men from the village. Yamrot said nothing. She never said anything. The days were always short, but during the rainy season they seemed even shorter. We had only two oil lamps, which lengthened our shadows on the adobe walls. Alamnew wasn't happy that she was still cooking, and he gave her a slap that knocked the pot to the ground with its force. I didn't yet know how to hold back my tears. With an urge to protect her that by then was second nature, Getachew and I inserted ourselves between our mother and that man, who seemed like a stranger. I had inherited his name as a surname: Alamnew. In Ethiopia, the names of fathers become surnames. From that time on, all men would scare me. And later I'd see that Yamrot never had any luck with men.

After the incident, Yamrot left with Getachew for her brother's house in Wereta, leaving me behind for a time that is hazy now. I remember only that Alamnew was living with another woman. Maybe he'd started a new family without us? Or maybe it was his sister or a cousin who was caring for him? I spent the days grazing the sheep and caring for two of that woman's children. I was like her *serratenya*, her maid.

I hated that place and that woman who would always scream at me, one of her children in her arms, glued to her breast, while she was busy leaving a pail at the door to collect rainwater. I never saw her laugh. The house was divided in two: they'd built a little adobe wall to separate the kitchen area from the room where we all slept. It was surrounded by cornfields and on rainy days I liked muddying my feet by running through the rows of corn plants, whacking the leaves so the droplets of water would splash my face.

When our neighbours planted cereals, I'd help sow the seeds in the ground while a man pulled the wooden plough, tilling the farmland. Yes, the plough was made of wood. What I liked best was the feel of the chickpea leaf: I would put a leaf on my tongue to feel how the skin crumbled. And keep crushing the chickpea leaf with my teeth.

ก

But Yamrot hadn't abandoned me under the shade of the *warka*. One day she came with Getachew to collect me from my father's house. It was the last time I saw Alamnew. I could see she was different, more confident than before. She was wearing the dress she always wore, the one I liked so much. A cotton dress, fitted at the waist with a band, it had a sky-blue background and flowers I remember sometimes as white and sometimes as dark grey. She had a bundle tied to her back. We went to Wereta that same day. On the way we made a stop at natural caves with thermal springs. The vapours made me feel sick. Yamrot insisted we plunge in. The water was full of grown-ups and sick people who had gone there in an attempt to be cured. As a little girl I'd seen practices that I now know were ancient and the basis of traditional medicine. I remember perfectly how a Wereta doctor would mark the back of a patient with the mouth of a very hot glass, leaving a piece of cotton inside for a while.

Yamrot, Getachew and I settled down in a small square adobe house with an asbestos roof on the outskirts of Wereta, where Yamrot had decided to build a future with us on her own, next to some rice fields. A plain that was always green, with pools of water. In the mornings we'd see the peasants coming down from the mountains to sell their goods at the market. In the house next door there lived a woman who would stay over in our house when Yamrot had to go away for some reason I wasn't aware of. There were days when she would go to the market of some surrounding town and come back with sweets for us. She kept them in her handbag and they'd smell of birr notes. Wereta was where we had the most: the house for three (and our neighbour, four) and a brown cow that we later sold.

Then Yamrot got pregnant, and I would never know by whom.

When Mikaele was born a few months later in Wereta, one night during the dry season, I went running to tell our neighbour so she could help with the birth. That night, Yamrot, our neighbour and I, still a little girl, brought Mikaele into the world: safe and sound but with no guarantee of a future.

✝

Around then, Yamrot made a lot of *dabo*, a small round bread that she would often sell from our house, in an alleyway that led straight to the market. The smell of freshly made *dabo* enchanted me, but whenever I tried to grab one before leaving to run errands, I'd find out to my disappointment that she'd counted them.

During the *Enkutatash* festivities Yamrot and her neighbours would paint each other's hands with a kind of henna, sitting around a pot in which a vegetable similar to beetroot was bubbling. When they had strained it, they would take the tuber, rub it on their hands and put it back into the pot, repeating the action until their whole hands were painted purple. The designs weren't as intricate and well defined as those created by the women in Harar in south-east Ethiopia, but they were festive enough. Local children would go out to gather yellow flowers and receive rewards, usually birrs, *dabo* or some other small token, after singing songs, traditional and religious. When it got dark, we would light a great torch and everyone would come together, singing before the flames. Wrapped in my *netela*, I was moved by the rhythm of the drums that hung from the young men's necks, the way they jumped offbeat; the sound throbbed in my chest.

፨

One day a man I'd never seen before came looking for Getachew. He left the Wereta house where we lived after the Ethiopian New Year festivities, which begin on 11 September and finish three days later. New Year also marks the end of the rainy season and the beginning of the harvest of the fields. I'm still not sure whether Getachew and I shared the same father. When you recall memories and wear them out, they're somehow rewritten. There are many details of my childhood that perhaps I'll never know for certain. I'll always be missing a few coats of paint.

፯

Yamrot made me suffer, made me feel very insecure. But I've returned to her image at every stage of my life. In her absence, my memory of her has served as a link to my country of origin. I've filled in the collage of information that connects Yamrot with all the women still living in the same way today, in the same economic and social conditions as her, convinced that in this way I would come to understand her. Yamrot had survived the Ethiopian civil war, was part of a generation that for the first time saw a democratic, prosperous future for themselves and their children. She was very young but, unfortunately, would never benefit from the positive changes.

During the political reforms of 1991, the Ethiopian government led by Meles Zenawi tried to adapt communist development policies and introduce a decentralised economic system to increase the growth and efficiency of the economy and thereby improve the standard of living of its citizens. Ethiopia's wealth comes mainly from the agrarian sector, and reforms were proposed to improve production and performance. According to the statistics published by Abiy Ahmed's government, in 2020 poverty in the country reduced at a rate directly proportional to economic growth. It is true that during the leadership of prime minister Hailemariam Desalegn, who was in power from 2012 to 2018, economic development had led to democratic stagnation, and Abiy Ahmed's political reform was a breath of fresh air for a society wanting to break with the repressive political tradition that had characterised previous governments and political regimes. But, according to studies by independent organisations, the poor of the 1990s became poorer still. Country people did not benefit from the economic reforms, or from the mechanisms that balance wages and prosperity, because Ethiopia wasn't industrialising at a rate that allowed it to go from being a society sustained by a rural workforce to being a society that, through the introduction of technology to the fields, improved the efficiency of the agrarian sector.

Illiteracy (more prevalent among women) prevents active participation in decision-making that defines the destiny and direction of a country. If there is no infrastructure to connect towns, there are no buses to bring children to school. Over the previous thirty years, and especially during the development of the UN Millennium Development Goals, Ethiopia had managed to increase the number of schools and informal study spaces, but still had issues of education quality and equal access to secondary schools. Girls were most affected by the lack of infrastructure. Good transport networks facilitate access to educational institutions for girls who live on the outskirts of cities or in sparsely populated areas. Where there are fewer economic resources, there is

less opportunity for girls to go to school. The lack
of a good education and work results in stagnation
and large-scale migration from rural areas to urban
areas. It is devastating.

The socialist Ethiopian revolution of the 1970s,
which marked the end of the feudal system and the
birth of the modern state of Ethiopia, was one of the
most important and successful in the world. Its motto
was '*Meret le arashu*': 'Land to the tiller'. However,
the adoption of communist ideology in Ethiopia
didn't generate the expected results, and only half
solved the problems of national identity. Because of
the Eurocentric nature of the European educational
and cultural system, none of this is well known, its
importance underestimated.

Writers and journalists from the Ethiopian diaspora have dedicated much time to understanding
these dynamics, and the implications of this revolution on daily life in urban and rural populations. For
example, Maaza Mengiste, in her novel *Beneath the
Lion's Gaze*, describes the repression of underground
student movements, the great land reform and the
implementation of the new system of administration
designed to control the populace even at the lowest
administrative level. Today, land rights still haven't
been reformed, and they are one of the reasons behind
the identity and internal border conflicts that place
Ethiopia among the countries with the highest level

of forced internal migration, sometimes of entire communities.

The empowering of Ethiopian women in the countryside, a project that has been brewing since the revolution of the 1970s, has not yet borne fruit. Although Abiy Ahmed's government introduced liberal policies and restructured parliament to make it 50 per cent women (with the first female president, Sahle-Work Zewde), such changes have been much slower and more difficult to introduce in rural areas, where tradition despises Western feminist values. The project of emancipating rural women still hasn't succeeded. Unless the education system in rural areas is extended, the patriarchal system and the traditions sustaining it cannot be broken.

There are many Ethiopian women of the diaspora who use their position to do their bit for the development of Ethiopia. Model and actress Liya Kebede is one of them. Her foundation, the Partnership for Maternal, Newborn and Child Health, collaborates with local organisations to reduce infant mortality in Africa. I discovered her while watching the film *Desert Flower,* based on the true story of Waris Dirie, a Somali model who fights to eradicate female genital mutilation.

Many international organisations have shown that if the economic resources of families living in the countryside are increased, the level of illiteracy among women decreases, and they stop emigrating to seek work opportunities elsewhere. Families with few economic resources don't have to marry women off to solve their difficulties and therefore gender-based violence is reduced.

Observing all these indicators of social development, I realised that Ethiopia is a country of contrasts: there is economic development, but it only benefits those who are already rich; there is educational development, but only as far as the outskirts of big cities; there is industrialisation, but it doesn't generate enough jobs for a country with a high volume of manpower. There are many other similar examples.

WE NEVER GOT HOME

Our nomadism brought us to Dansha, the small city in the west of Tigray that is a crossroads, a gateway. The bus left us in the centre, in front of the clothes market. We got there at midday. It was very hot and my braids burned if I touched them.

The Dansha clothes market was a place that fascinated me. Men and women shouting, displaying patterned fabrics of all colours, a labyrinth of small stalls so close together that everything seemed to be made of cloth. You couldn't see where one stall began and the next ended. In the afternoons, when I went to do errands for Yamrot, I'd see street vendors weighed down with the fabrics and dresses that hung from their arms, moving in front of the bars and little restaurants where one song mingled with another. The melody of Teddy Afro's first record clashed with the melody of a song by Haimanot Girma. Yamrot and I had only three dresses each: two floral ones which we would alternate, and a *kemis*, the traditional white dress that we would wear on special occasions and religious celebrations. We chose the fabrics for the newest ones from among the labyrinth and carried them to a tailor: they took our measurements and after a week had made up the dresses for us. Yamrot wore her new dress to work, as a cleaning lady in a house. She stopped taking me there with her because I touched everything and sometimes would even snatch birrs I found hidden around the house (Ethiopia is one of the countries with the lowest use of and access to banks). I knew we were short of money and I wasn't ashamed to take it if I saw it.

When it seemed that we would be staying in Dansha, I told Yamrot I wanted to go to school. She told me I could go when I could touch my left ear with the fingers of my right hand, with my arm passing over my head. And, like previous generations, who used historic events (like a war) or natural events (like a drought) to define people's birth dates, I waited patiently to grow.

At that time, Yamrot was working in the *bunna bet* of the grandmother of a girl named Tigist. I wanted to do exactly what Tigist was doing: dress well and go to school. Above all, I wanted to learn to read and write. Tigist was taller than me; she must have been a few years older. I'd often wait for her to come home with her classmates. Yamrot tried to get the idea out of my head but, like her, I was stubborn, and she ended up buying me a small notebook with blue-striped pages and a pencil. One morning I walked to the school, following a group of children who were also on their way there. It was on top of a hill, on the outskirts of Dansha, towards Eritrea. I entered the enclosure, which was surrounded by green-painted walls. There were four low buildings, single-storey, and from outside you could see into the rooms. As I'd heard Tigist do so many times, I sang the 'flag anthem' with all the other pupils while they lined up in the middle of the yard to begin the school day. Camouflaged among the students, I determinedly entered the room I believed should be mine. Everything was going well. I'd already used my notebook and pencil for the first time, trying to copy some phrases in Amharic from the blackboard. Amharic is a Semitic language and is the only language on the whole of sub-Saharan Africa that has its own alphabet. Suddenly, the teacher called the register and my name wasn't there. My heart was beating very fast. I was an impostor and they'd caught me. The teacher told me that to attend classes I'd need to register and pay for enrolment. I never went back. Yamrot didn't have enough money to enrol me in school as we lived from hand to mouth. So that is why until the age of seven I had only been to school for one day. I only knew how to write my name in Amharic because Yamrot had taught me.

Yamrot knew how to read and write, the bare minimum. But there were women who didn't and had to use their fingerprint to sign documents or participate in local elections.

ፆ

Nelson Mandela once said: 'Education is the most powerful weapon which you can use to change the world.' But how can the world be changed if a girl like I once was wants to go to school and be educated but cannot? How can one try to change the world when such a high percentage of global society is illiterate, lives outside the digital footprint and faces a constant struggle to survive because its basic needs such as water, electricity and housing are not met?

ፇ

Mikaele slept while we stretched out on the floor of the house with an asbestos roof and walls of wooden logs and mud, which at night made us feel too close to the hyenas as they squealed and rummaged for a distracted chicken or for a scrap of meat. It was completely empty of furniture and belongings, other than a single bed made from a goatskin mattress tied to wooden legs and a small cupboard with kitchen utensils. Yamrot told me that she had a sister who had left to study abroad. She told me that I looked very like my aunt. Speaking of her and how she'd left home, she peered through the open door that looked onto a street illuminated by the midday sun and fell silent. She left out many of the worries, frustrations and desires that a seven-year-old girl would never be able to understand. That sister of hers became for me like a crack that let in a ray of sunshine. My world could expand as far as that land where an aunt supposedly lived. From then on, my eyes began to follow the trajectory and white-coloured trails of the aeroplanes in the sky. Large buses with wings. The relationship between my grandparents and Yamrot seemed not to have been good. They had taken her out of school and married her off while she was still a teenager. Her surname was Egigayew, the name of her father. She was actually named Yemata, which means 'she of the night'. She was Yemata Egigayew, but everyone called her Yamrot. Her parents lived in Debre Tabor and Yamrot told me that they had taken care of me when I was very small, while she and Alamnew worked in the fields during the day. But I don't remember that at all.

ከ

One afternoon, having left Tigist's grandmother's *bunna bet* when the sun started to go down, casting part of Dansha city into shadow, Yamrot gathered our few belongings: a pot, three plates, two *netelas*. I'd seen her do the same thing when we lived in Wereta. This time, too, she'd decided that we needed to seek out a new opportunity. In fact, it had never been difficult for us to leave. We hadn't put roots down anywhere and we only had each other.

Yamrot had met a man in the cafe who suggested travelling to Humera to cook for a group of cotton pickers in the fields on both sides of the road that linked Dansha and Humera. As the lights of the restaurants and bars at the edge of the road began to come on, music would blare from inside, and people from the little towns would gather around the trucks and dusty buses to go back to their houses. We climbed up on top of a truck full of men and some women, and drove away from the city. From the top of the trailer, Dansha looked flat and ever smaller, surrounded by bushes that filled the landscape. The shouts of people pushing each other to grab a seat on top of the trucks had suddenly stopped and a dense silence enveloped us. Yamrot, Mikaele and I sat close together, with a *netela* to protect us from the wind and sand. The driver of the truck had turned on the radio, and a song in Tigrinya – the official language of Tigray and Eritrea – could be heard mingling with the voices of the people sitting in the trailer and the sound of the engine. The journey took a few hours.

We stopped at the gates of Humera, which was surrounded by desert land.

ሐ

Cotton has been produced and used in Ethiopia since
ancient times. In 2019, Ethiopia had eighty thousand
hectares of land reserved for cultivating cotton. Since
2015, the Ethiopian government had been trying to
increase the productivity of the cotton yield through
the Growth and Transformation Plan. Developing the
textile sector to create new jobs was a project that was
part of the then-government's ambition to convert
Ethiopia into the primary producer of cotton in the
world within the next twelve years, producing more
than a million metric tonnes of cotton annually. This
would mean creating more industrial estates around
the country and increasing international investment
in the textile sector.

ሸ

Days in the fields were long and hot. From the moment
the sun came up until it set, we would pick bolls of
cotton and put them into a polyester bag decorated
with the colours of the Ethiopian flag: *aranguadi*,
bitcha, *kay*. Green, yellow, red. We'd share one bag
between two or three people. While Yamrot prepared

the various meals of the day for the collectors, I'd tie
Mikaele to my back with a *netela* crossed at the breast
and help the group fill the sack. When the sun was
scorching, we would sit under the tents made from the
same fabric as the bags, held up with four posts, until
the wind started up again, and then we would go back
to gathering cotton until the evening. When it grew
dark we would sit under the stars around the fire that
lit up the dense black night, and the seasonal workers
would tell anecdotes and sing, raising up their voices
despite their fatigue. For many, like us, that place was
new; but others came year after year to plant cotton
or pick it. The cotton was still spun manually, with
a wooden spindle. I'd seen the neighbours do it and
I'd learned how to do it in the same way I'd learned
to sew: by repetition. I liked seeing how we moved
in a slow yet constant rhythm, emptying the field of
white to restore it to its pure green hue. Often Yamrot
would take part in the gathering and the two of us
would fill our hands with bolls of cotton and empty
them into the same sack. Wanting to finish quickly,
I'd grab the bolls badly and scratch my fingers. Tied
to my back, Mikaele would be lulled to sleep with the
swaying of my body, indifferent to our labour. And
when he couldn't sleep, I'd walk up and down around
the field, moving towards and away from the group
of collectors until he stopped moaning. When I felt
his head resting on the back of my neck, I knew he'd

fallen asleep. I've always said I worked in the cotton fields with my mother. Even though we were only there for a few weeks, that stay just outside Humera would shape me and be one of the many jobs I saw Yamrot do to be able to feed us. I didn't know what dictated our movements, whether it was us or the jobs, but it seemed we'd never stop being nomads.

CD

Once the cotton was picked, all three of us got onto another truck on the outskirts of Humera and returned to Dansha. After the Fasika celebrations, the symptoms of Yamrot's illness began to appear and she lost the vital energy that was so much a part of her. In a very short time, she no longer had the drive to arrange and decide day-to-day things. Her decline took us by surprise. Yamrot went to talk to a neighbour who knew about illnesses. She told her she must have been infected by a lizard. I don't know if Yamrot believed her or not, but, just in case, I always covered all the food in the house so no animal could get near it – maybe that woman was right. I'd often go to pray in the Orthodox church in Dansha with my white cotton *netela* with grey and silver stripes covering my braids; with my blue floral made-to-measure dress and my black plastic shoes. I'd kiss the holy stone wall of the Orthodox church and kneel on my skinny knees. I'd stay with my forehead touching the ground for quite some time, while in the distance the call to prayer from the muezzin of a mosque could be heard. I thought Yamrot being unwell was my fault.

Unsolved trauma can be triggered by different sensory elements in very unexpected ways. If there's a film that explains many of the feelings I experienced as a little girl arriving in Catalonia, it's *Va, vis et deviens* (*Live and Become*) by Radu Mihăileanu. Even though it takes place in the 1980s in Israel, there are scenes that move me deeply today: the main character, an Ethiopian boy aged seven or eight called Solomon, adopted by an Israeli family, getting out of a comfortable bed in the middle of the night to sleep on the floor instead; or trying to cover the plug of the shower with his little hands, horrified by the quantity of water draining away. He has to adjust to his new reality while dealing with the deprivations he endured in a refugee camp in Sudan during Operation Moses, in which the United States and Israel, in collaboration with the Sudanese military, sent thousands of Ethiopian Jews from Sudan to Israel in forty-five days. He, an Orthodox Christian, pretending to be a Falasha, ends up in a Jewish family; I would end up in an atheist family at his age. For me it was very difficult to learn to choose. I didn't know how. When I hadn't been in Catalonia very long, if we went into a bakery and I was asked to choose what I wanted as a snack (a regular croissant or a chocolate one, or a piece of cake…) I'd end up asking them to buy me whatever; and if they insisted that I choose, I would run out of the shop without anything at all. I found it very frustrating that there was so much choice and that they let me choose when Yamrot hadn't been able to do so. It's not that there weren't options in Ethiopia; there were. But we didn't have the privilege of being able to choose, in the same way that in 2003 in many corners of Europe a large number of families didn't either. Essentially, my dilemma was accepting to what point I could enjoy the freedom I hadn't had with Yamrot.

Yamrot's illness came suddenly, and to stay. Like a cloud that seemed to hover over us alone. When she'd been sick for weeks, lying down, with no energy for anything, the only thing she could do was clutch Mikaele to her right breast while she squeezed the other, checking which of her two breasts, as dry as her whole body, could give more milk. My little brother was three years old, but as we had so little food, and he didn't have the strength to chew, Yamrot would try to give him the sparse milk she had left. I'd suddenly become older. I'd go shopping in the market and cook what she told me to: almost always it was *shiro* or boiled pumpkin. We ate very little *doro*, chicken. With no one to worry about me, I'd stroll the streets of Dansha alone, under the weight of the burning sun amid the dense silence of the midday streets; or I'd climb the tamarind trees, eating their fruit. I didn't have girlfriends, I didn't have boyfriends. It wasn't possible, because we never managed to stay at any address long enough. I'd observed with scorn that among children there were codes reminiscent of our parents, their insecurities, their political ideologies… If I didn't come back with my head bleeding from being hit by a small stone, I'd come back held by the ear by one of the neighbourhood mothers, her daughter bearing a scratched face. There were also moments of discovery: I remember grabbing a cigarette stub from the floor, still alight, and imitating the gestures of smokers, or stealing a mango or an orange from a street stall; sometimes I'd join a group of children and we'd run through the unpaved streets until our hearts were coming out of our mouths. Barefoot, my black plastic shoes in my hand, because they made my feet sweat and gave me blisters. So many blisters that the scars are still visible. They are the marks of my past.

I no longer knew how to take care of Mikaele, who would cry from hunger at night. When he was born, Yamrot and I seemed to shift from being mother and daughter to sharing his upbringing, as well as some of the responsibilities of the house. My little brother stole a large portion of my childhood innocence. Through slaps and very severe rules I learned the value of the things we could have and those we couldn't. One morning I'd gone to buy three eggs and, in a hurry to get home, I was running with the eggs in a little plastic bag when I tripped on a stone and the eggs and I fell flat on the earthen road. Yamrot's response was blunt: she hit me so hard I couldn't feel my cheek. I'd learned that when she raised her hand, I had to take the blow and let the tears fall. I had no choice or means of escape. It was her way of teaching me, one lesson after another.

Yamrot was a solitary person who focused on the jobs she could do to move forward and care for us as far as possible. Sometimes she had 'guests': men who would come and go. What a nerve! They'd come to our house, disturb our routine and leave – and all for some birrs that were never enough. I learned quickly about the objectification of women. I watched helplessly as all the strength Yamrot had gained on leaving Alamnew was called into question when, late at night, a drunk man I didn't know would knock on the door of the modest house with the asbestos roof. Or when I'd wake up in the early hours with a man between my mother and me, a man who had decided not to leave even though she was insisting in a firm voice that he go. It seemed as if quarrels and the violence of men followed us.

0

When Anna and Ricard asked me about Yamrot in 2003, still in Addis Ababa with Kumbi and Teddy acting as interpreters from Amharic, I didn't say anything about these episodes in our lives. With hindsight, I realise that I selected the things I thought I could tell and those I couldn't. I told them about the streets, the jokes I'd heard, the values I'd learned, the respect for adults that had been instilled in me, and about religion. But then instinctively I wanted to protect Yamrot's image. I didn't want to say anything that might denigrate her. In essence, mothers who aren't with us are somewhere between imagination, idealisation and nostalgia. They have the power to be redeemed, like the phoenix that rises from its own ashes.

I could see that it didn't matter how painful whatever I was explaining was; my words had gravitas. Everyone was impressed by my replies. I wondered when a girl stops being a girl on one side of the world and when on the other. If knowing all the techniques for lighting a fire with just a single match impressed them, maybe it was better to wait before explaining the facts that I'd known since I was very small were taboo, those that never reached the public space for debate, the *bunna bet*. The subjects that formed a lump in my throat. Little by little, over time, I'd also leave male violence and my fear of men behind. But I always stayed alert.

I rarely spoke of Yamrot; maybe the person who spoke about her most, who wanted to know most about her, was Anna, who made sure from the beginning I wouldn't forget her. She made me tell her what I remembered of Yamrot, she made me draw her. Because I didn't have a single photo of my mother, during the first trip back to Ethiopia, Anna began to take pictures of women who might look like her (by dint of their hairstyles, their clothes, their ages…). She always said that I had two mothers now: Yamrot, who was no longer there, and her. I too always wanted Yamrot's efforts and everything she had done to establish the foundations of my manners to be recognised. People would often tell Ricard and Anna that I was a very polite little girl, and one day I told them: 'Don't think it's all because of you! Yamrot taught me lots of things too!'

H

In the forming of identity, and especially in what is called 'socially constructed identity', ties are forged over time. Links of recognition. I was the link between Yamrot and Anna. Anna was the link between all the women that had preceded her and me: my grandmother Teresa, my great-grandmother Lu (short for Lucrècia), my great-great-grandmother Angelina… Through life's twists, of all of them I was the one who attained the highest level of education, even though my grandmother Teresa was the first woman in her family to go to university, and my mother Anna was the first woman to have her own company. Anna was raised by parents who, like so many others in 1970s Catalonia, had climbed the social ladder to move from working class to university-attending middle class.

When Anna was two, my grandfather Joan began a degree in medicine in Barcelona as a mature student, having worked since being orphaned as an adolescent. My grandfather studied and worked at the same time and my grandmother was a teacher in a good, non-religious, mixed private school that followed the Montessori model of education. The four children they had were able to study there on scholarships, thanks to her being one of the teachers.

Of all the women who have preceded me, the one with whom I feel the strongest connection, without having known her, is my great-grandmother Lu, who died the very year I was born, in 1996. Lu had to leave school at the age of nine to work in a Sabadell textile factory, using her small hands among the turn-of-the-century looms, and to help out at home, where she had many siblings. The bond I have with all these women is as strong as a biological link and I'm moved by how a thread of self-improvement, resilience and ambition can be traced back, generation after generation. Time improves women's standard of living and will improve it further still if we create opportunities for the girls of the future. I've learned many things from my experience, but the most important is that we need to give girls the necessary tools to enable them to fully realise their potential in life.

ℋ

Neighbours in Dansha would ask me how Yamrot was and I'd respond by saying she was very well, getting better. But the truth was that Yamrot was declining at a dizzying rate, and I held back so as not to anger her and to try to lessen her moans of pain. I was beginning to realise the gravity of our situation and I didn't know who I should ask for help. Not that we knew how to ask for help either because, if we did… what were we doing so far from home?

Everything happened very quickly. Very early one morning, Yamrot, Mikaele and I boarded a bus going south, which ended its journey in Gondar. We went with only what we were wearing, nothing else. We were on our way home, to Wereta. Yamrot must have known that she had very little time left. She was very weak.

On the bus, which was chock-full of people and moving very slowly, it was very hot and there was a lot of noise. There were many potholes on the dry, unpaved earth road and the driver had to brake constantly if he didn't want to overturn. I was sitting beside the window, with Mikaele on my lap. Yamrot was sitting by the aisle. A couple was carrying some chickens tied together by their feet. Entire families were sitting on top of one another, filling the whole space. The dirty glass windows were lowered, but the dust rising from the road and the black smoke from the bus itself made it impossible to breathe deeply. When the road was no longer so straight and I saw bends ahead of us, I began to feel a little calmer. I looked out and imagined my days in Wereta. I wondered how my uncles were, and if Getachew, my brother, was already back with them. When we lived in Wereta I used to run from the market to the house of Yamrot's brother and his wife, who was called Kalkidan, and shout her name loudly from the railings of the little garden. She would come out to open the grille in front of the door so I could enter with a plastic bag full of lemons and limes. Kalkidan had told me that lemon was very good for stopping my uncle's nosebleeds. I always used to see him sitting in the shade, looking out at the street, inspecting passing life; he was a friendly-looking man of few words.

They were our family in Wereta and I was eager to see them again after so many months or years – I'd lost all notion of time. What was time for me then? In Wereta I'd begun to perceive the magnitude of space and time. During the rainy season, the most entertaining activity was to find the rainiest, muddiest street and slide, on my bottom, often on a piece of plastic bag, with the kids of the neighbourhood. Or build bridges over little streams, one beside the other, all the boys and girls with muddy hands, with no idea of proportion, balance or depth. We loved seeing the water running under our bridges, carrying away whatever couldn't withstand the flow and force of the current.

And during the dry season we would gather guavas from the tree. On the hottest days, I'd run up the deserted street with a coin in my sweaty palm until I reached a *suk* and on tiptoes in front of the small shop I'd ask for a homemade orange ice cream, held by two toothpicks. Yamrot would never give me more money than that single coin and I already knew that I could only buy myself an ice cream or two *mastica*, the rectangular chewing gums sold singly and not in packets.

Yamrot's cough brought me down from the clouds. To a reality that was more and more difficult for me to handle or face. Mikaele, sitting on my lap, had a fever. We were already close to Gondar: the bus took a sharp bend and Yamrot vomited again and also wet herself. The passengers around us made grimaces of disgust as they turned away, covering their noses with their *netela*s or any other scrap of clothing they had to hand. Yamrot, wrapped in her *netela* which by now was more brown than white and covered in bloodstains, wiped her mouth, avoiding the stares, her sight lost to the horizon. She no longer had the strength for anything. Everyone understood that she was very sick, and pitied us – they'd surely seen many families like ours – but no one said anything. In fact, it seemed as though the one they most pitied was me, given that I was the only one of the three who could still endure their staring. I was ashamed. Mikaele was so weak that he hadn't cried or asked for food for hours: he was dehydrated and malnourished.

I tried to shut out the situation by thinking about the good times the three of us had had together. The thought that we had left Wereta so full of life and were now returning on the brink of death was hard for me. I was acutely aware that living without Yamrot would mean no one to bring food home. It made me dizzy. I remembered the films I'd seen in Tigist's grandmother's *bunna bet* in Dansha, when Yamrot was working there as a cook. In the *bunna bet*, which was right by the road, there was a little television and a video player where they'd play music videos and films. Amid the chaos of the bus I couldn't help but think about a scene in one film where a group of delinquents stopped a bus and boarded it to rob the passengers of their money and jewellery. Beforehand, however, the passengers had taken off their rings and necklaces and hidden them in their mouths or in their clothing. The armed men stopped in front of one young woman and carried her off to rape her in the middle of the wood, but she managed to escape and run towards the road. Unexpectedly, a woman picked her up in her car and took her to Addis Ababa.

It wasn't strange that such images came to mind: they were talked about by the people of the *bunna bet* and mingled with stories and real events to prevent children straying from home. But they were ultimately images of the reality left by the civil war, in which armed groups had taken control and survived by holding up and threatening peasants. On the roads north of Dansha you risked being robbed at gunpoint and getting stuck there, with no money and no wheels on the vehicle.

While I waited for Yamrot to finish her working day in the Dansha *bunna bet*, I'd spend hours hypnotised in front of the television, watching everything, with no filter. That place attracted many people, above all men, and especially truck drivers on the road to Humera and the border with Eritrea, or to Sudan. UN soldiers who had been sent to the Humera base would also spend time there. It hadn't been long since the war with Eritrea had ended, and despite the attempt to consolidate the peace in a treaty signed in Algiers in 2000, where a commission to demarcate an official border between Ethiopia and Eritrea was established, Ethiopia had decided not to accept the conditions of the treaty and both countries had entered a state of 'not war and not peace', which meant that from time to time violence would erupt between the two sides. When we lived in Dansha, the border with Eritrea was closed and guarded by Ethiopian soldiers. My body would become tense all over when I saw the soldiers.

The second job Yamrot had found in Dansha was cleaning a hotel that became a brothel by night. While Yamrot worked, Mikaele and I would stay with the owner of the hotel. One evening a group of men wearing military uniforms arrived. And some of the women, including Yamrot, left with them. I didn't understand what went on in that hotel and I cried myself to sleep, tired of waiting for her.

Yamrot wasn't an easy woman; she had character. Once she had a fist fight with a work colleague, and not only did she lose a front tooth, but she was taken to the police station, where she was detained for a few hours, which seemed an eternity to me. Maybe it was days? I didn't understand that either. I went back to stay with Mikaele and the hotel owner until Yamrot came to get us and we settled down in a little house on the other side of the city, close to Tigist's grandmother's *bunna bet*. It would be a time of stability for the three of us, despite the precariousness of our situation. Yamrot would cook at Tigist's grandmother's *bunna bet* and, with nothing else to do, I'd often watch her. In the back there was a door that led to a little shack, with walls made of logs and a roof of branches, where she'd cook the *injera* in a wood-burning oven. She'd tie a *netela* at her waist, which she would use to wipe the sweat from her brow; when she removed the lid, hot steam billowed out of the *injera* and it would be very hot in there. She would put sunflower or sesame oil on a cloth and spread it over the clay plate, then she would fill a plastic pot with the *injera*'s liquid dough from the pail at her side. Carefully controlling the movement of her wrist, she'd cover the clay plate with the dough, making ever-bigger circles from the centre outwards, until she finally had a single piece of dough in the shape of a circle, like a crêpe. I'd be looking on, taking care not to distract her and watching how next she'd cover the clay plate with a metal or sometimes ceramic cone, and she'd go over the edge of the clay plate again with a cloth already darkened with use, so the heat didn't escape. Not using a timer, she'd uncover the clay plate and, with a raffia tray, lift the *injera* little by little and pull it out in one piece. She'd pile up the *injera*s, cover them with another cloth to keep them warm and repeat the process all over again. One *injera* after another. And always aware of the fire, adding more logs of dry eucalyptus wood and fanning them.

Maybe one of the clearest examples of our precarious economic situation was when my black plastic shoe fell into a latrine. I had to balance so as not to fall in, as it was big enough to see everything, even the worms. Between shouting and pinching my arm, Yamrot grabbed a stick and brought me to the edge of the hole. I thought she would beat me. We could see the shoe floating in the shit. She lowered the stick into the hole and fished out the shoe. Utterly focused, we paid no heed to the stench or the flies. The shoe was more important, because she couldn't buy me another.

ፀ

When we left Wereta that unexpected morning, telling no one we were going, we walked to the bus station. We would begin our journey north by taking the bus to Gondar, which meant waiting until first light, the three of us – Yamrot, Mikaele and me – lying on the ground. There were other families and old people sleeping out in the open. As well as an empty bus with closed doors, there were trucks and military vehicles. I remember the feel of the cool earth beneath my bare feet as we walked through the unusually deserted streets. Also a poster advertising a brand of biscuits that was everywhere then. I stared at it for a long time that early morning, trying to sleep a little more, lying in a corner of that bus station. It was a photo of a traditional family: the father was clutching a daughter by her hand and the mother was clutching a son by his. In a way such a typical image, it was also social indoctrination into what an ideal family was. People could live in precarious circumstances, spending long rainy seasons with frugal meals by candlelight, forever in cold damp, but the image of the wealthy family persisted as a core value. Poverty and wealth side by side.

Those images also made me think that perhaps neither Getachew nor Alamnew would ever be part of our lives again. In Ethiopia, at the time of my childhood, when a couple separated, daughters would go with their father to continue doing household tasks, and sons would stay with the mother to help her with the other tasks it was assumed only a man could do. But Yamrot had broken all those stereotypes. She had left Wereta for an unknown place in the north, with very little by way of savings and a heavy burden: a little girl clutching her hand and an even littler boy tied to her back. None of her children were registered. We weren't listed on any census. Officially we didn't exist. We were undocumented inside our own country, we couldn't claim any governmental responsibility for our needs. It was (and remains) 'save yourselves' for those who belonged to the poorest sector of Ethiopian society.

ℓ

Now we were going back to Wereta, but Yamrot was coughing more and more blood onto her *netela*. Very worried, I was watching her and wondering what I would do when we got to Gondar to find the next bus. It wasn't so far to our final destination, where I could let myself fall into the arms of my uncle and his wife. They would take care of Yamrot and Mikaele, there was nothing a warm *enkulal firfir* with tomato and onion, like Kalkidan used to make, couldn't cure. I could already smell the sauce soaking the *injera*.

From the bus window I finally saw that yes, we were arriving in Gondar. We came into the bus station in the city centre in the light of the afternoon sun, but didn't move from our seats until everyone else got off. The driver was furious. He screamed at us for leaving the bus in such a state. He and another driver helped us down. In fact, they pretty well dragged us and threw us roughly at the bus stop. Yamrot's body fell like a bag of bones to the ground; she didn't even have the strength to walk. I tied Mikaele to my back with a *netela*. I hadn't eaten or drunk anything for many hours and I was exhausted by the journey, the bus's constant shuddering over roads either badly paved or not paved at all. I was completely disoriented and Yamrot was no longer speaking.

Shortly before our bus was to leave, once again full of passengers who watched us without offering us any help, a local police car appeared. A dying woman and two small children prone on the ground with no baggage at all drew attention, especially in a place full of busy people struggling to board a *bajaj* to get home before dark. To avoid accidents, the government had passed a law to reduce nocturnal traffic rather than improve the condition of the roads. There were boys and girls my age trying to sell the rest of the *kolo* they had left in their wooden bowls and packets of tissues. Two police officers got out of the car and came over to ask where we were going. They tried to speak to Yamrot but she had neither voice nor will to answer. She had reached her limit. It seemed the journey had accelerated the progress of her sickness. I was crying uncontrollably because of the situation.

The two men helped settle us in the back seats of their official car and drove us to the outskirts of Gondar. I was sure that they would take us to Wereta, where I'd told them we were going, to our home. But they stopped the engine in front of a metallic door painted turquoise. The policemen got out of the car, leaving the three of us inside. They knocked on the door and it was opened by a woman wearing a strange white dress with blue trim of a kind I'd never seen before. I watched them from the window of the car, worried. They were talking, and from time to time they would gesture towards us. Finally, the two police-men and the woman in the strange white dress helped us out of the car and into that place. Yamrot was half-conscious and one of the policemen carried her in his arms. That man's uniform became covered in blood and vomit. Since I didn't know how, I couldn't read the painted sign at the entrance: MISSIONARIES OF CHARITY. It was one of the eighteen reception centres in Ethiopia belonging to the order founded by Teresa of Calcutta, one of more than a hundred around the world. That woman was wearing an Indian sari. Later I would learn that her name was Mariska. She was Sister Mariska.

The policemen left us there. Another missionary appeared with a piece of paper and a pen, very friendly and affectionate. She asked me our names, how old we were, where we had come from and where we were going. She wrote everything down as I answered. Two more women came over, dressed the same, and separated us. They took Yamrot to one of the low buildings which made up the centre where there were other sick women, one bed beside the next. They took Mikaele to the children's infirmary. And they took me to another small building where there were other healthy boys and girls, watched over by the cooks and the nuns themselves. The first night they let me sleep as long as I wanted. I could have slept for two days straight. Perhaps I did. The door of the dormitory was right next to the infirmary where they'd placed Mikaele and I could go to see him whenever I wanted.

Even though I felt like a caged bird, I found this centre run by the Calcutta missionaries very beautiful, and I'd never seen anywhere like it – it infused me with peace and security. When I wasn't visiting Yamrot or Mikaele I would stroll around the garden that connected all the buildings of the centre in a perfect square of cement. There was a white statue of the Virgin Mary that made quite an impression on me. When I passed before it, I'd press my fingers together like in the Romanesque pictures of Sant Climent de Taüll and put them first on my left shoulder, then on my right, then on my forehead, and I'd end by kissing my fingers. I was repeating a gesture I'd internalised, having seen it performed so many times in Orthodox churches in front of the image of the Virgin, who we called Mariam, and which I was doing now before that chalk sculpture painted white in a Catholic centre. It was how Yamrot and I would bless our food before we ate, in a quick, subtle gesture.

I would also sit, after I'd checked that Mikaele was asleep, on a stone bench that served as a railing in front of the infirmary, and stay there for hours watching how the gardener cared for the plants, especially the rose bushes. I'd never seen roses before. When they let me, I'd go with the carers to wash clothes in the river or go to the little study where the nuns did administrative tasks. Hanging on one wall was a framed photo of a woman already very old, dressed in the same way; they called her Mother Teresa. I played with the other boys and girls very little. I was very quiet and was always watching attentively what went on in the centre.

How many people like us did these women receive? The missionaries opened the turquoise door twice a day. There were always sick and dying people, wrapped in their white *netelas*, sitting outside, waiting for them to open. Once a week they would cook great pots of rice and lentils and go out to distribute the food to the people queueing in front of the door.

ON DUAL IDENTITY

I'm interested in the subject of identity. Above all, I'm interested in dual identity. I've grown up learning how to move between my Ethiopian and my Catalan identity, from my African heritage to my European.

I started my academic education in a Barcelona public school and I continued it in another public high school in the same neighbourhood of Gràcia. I was lucky in both primary school and secondary school to find some exceptional teachers, who taught me that with effort and perseverance anything is possible. Possible even if you've just arrived from Ethiopia at seven years old and you're illiterate. Although they had few resources, the teachers invested a lot of time and energy in giving me the tools to adapt as quickly as possible and made the most of my desire to learn.

I was also lucky to be able to share classrooms all through primary school with boys and girls from very different origins: there were fewer than thirty of us, with more than twenty nationalities between us. Having classmates and playmates from places as different as Senegal, Morocco, Brazil, China, Chile and Gràcia's gypsy community really helped me during my early years in Catalonia. It helped me to not feel so different, not stand out, not be in too much of a hurry and not want to erase my identity, because the teachers valued it and made us explain where we were from, which languages we spoke and what we would eat at home. Gràcia then wasn't like London, but it was as close as you could get to authentic diversity at school.

In my final years of adolescence, after spending a few weeks in New York (attending a music, film and drama camp for teenagers from around the world) and walking alone through a crowd of people of all races and origins, determined and confident on the streets of Brooklyn and Manhattan, I saw little by little that I'd outgrown the neighbourhood of Gràcia, the city of Barcelona and also the countryside of Castellterçol, where I spent a lot of time. I knew that my comfort zone might be beyond what I already knew. I believed that, like Yamrot, I too was a nomad. Broadening mindsets has always been important to me: we should all aspire to societies interconnected by people who have been educated in different cultures, by people who can act as bridges: between cultures, between languages, between ideologies. I realised that cultural diversity and inclusivity must surely help societies to become more just.

After some frustrating attempts to fit into the moulds society was offering me, I came to the conclusion that it is how you construct your identity, not how others see you, that is important. Tigray is significant to me, it's important to my identity, because I lived there and some of the most important memories of my childhood are rooted there. Besides this, I'm not Tigrayan but Amhara. How do we make places our own? How do we belong to places without being native to them?

Losing my original social environment has allowed me to see that we reproduce the traditions with which we've been in contact – a detail that is fundamental to understanding how nations form a collective identity. I've been consolidating the elements of Amhara identity on every one of my journeys back, and also through songs and what I've found on YouTube and on social media; I've found ways of practising Amharic and deepening my knowledge of Ethiopian customs. I can't contrast all this, a priori, with the other identities that make up Ethiopia. I was educated in Catalonia, a nation inside the Spanish state. When I travel around the world and say I'm from Barcelona, people's automatic response is to list Spanish stereotypes, with no reference to my Catalan culture. Because of the colour of my skin, I not only have to justify having a Spanish passport, but also have to refute the half-lies about my country: Catalonia.

The last time I went to Nairobi, a security guard from the Spanish embassy asked me where I'd got my surnames, Domingo Soler. 'I stole them, doesn't it bug you?' But I've never been quick-witted; I only thought it as I explained that my parents are Catalan. Often I avoid explaining who I am, but still I end up going through uncomfortable experiences like this. Or worse. For me, all this is key to understanding the cultural dominance that exists within multicultural states, especially in those that are a threat to minority languages and nations.

I've been able to observe that a satisfactory adoption is one in which both the child and parents mutually adopt each other's cultures of origin. I see it as a contract and I would say: if parents try to suppress or repress our identity and culture of origin, they are depriving us of the tools that help us understand our world, where we come from and why we are as we are. Then there is the process of putting down roots. I was adopted not only by my parents: my sister Lara and my brother Roger adopted me as soon as they met me, just as my cousins, aunts, uncles and grandparents did. With the perspective of time, I think that Lara has had a hugely important role in my putting down roots in Catalonia, and above all during my early twenties, when I started to spend a lot of time abroad because of my studies and early jobs. In fact, the whole family constantly keeps me rooted.

International adoptions often happen in homogeneous Western societies where families move away from immigrant networks in a counterproductive attempt to integrate their son or daughter and avoid their being stigmatised in the new community. Deculturalisation, an almost inevitable process that is considered normal in the international adoption sphere, is an act of deprivation; it removes the keys to integration, although it is intended, purportedly, to counter racism. As if the fact of acquiring awareness of racism might in itself be a form of rebellion against the new family and culture that have adopted you. On the other hand, because of our origin, we'll always be asked about the political or social situation in our country of origin with a meaningful look, as if we should be experts. A Muslim woman becomes an expert when there is a terrorist attack in Somalia or Syria; the Black woman must be an expert and able to give a detailed opinion when there is a demonstration asserting 'Black Lives Matter', and so on and so on.

With the aim of finding spaces where multiculturalism was not only a slogan but a reality, I studied for my entire Political Science degree at the University of Kent in England, with its campus situated between forests and green meadows on the outskirts of the city of Canterbury. It welcomed more than twenty-five thousand students from all over the world. At Josep Maria Jujol Primary School in Barcelona I was surrounded by boys and girls from very different backgrounds, but as I grew up, and especially on going to Vila de Gràcia Secondary School, which was just across the street, diversity was left behind. I remember comments made by Ricard and Anna and their concern (highly involved and active as they were in the parents' association, in primary school as well as secondary). The diversity in the secondary school classrooms wasn't the same – indeed very much less than – I'd experienced in the classrooms of my primary school. By the time I finished my high school diploma there was no longer any diversity at all: those of us who didn't have white skin could be counted on one hand. And the offspring of newly arrived immigrants were even fewer, an exception.

It shocks me when I think about it, because I would contend that the more educated you are, the more tools you have and the greater the possibility of achieving freedom. Curiously, one of the classmates who helped me most in the subjects that I found hardest was Ruoyi, the only Asian girl in my last year of high school. She had arrived from China at the age of seven, the same age that I arrived from Ethiopia. But, as with many other kids recently arrived in Catalonia, her parents couldn't help her to do her homework as my parents did me, because they didn't understand Catalan and barely understood Spanish. With the passing of time, I admire Ruoyi more and more and

I'll always be grateful to her for having shared her perseverance and resilience with me, in a system that excludes and puts many obstacles before those with few resources (because sometimes it's not only about the language) and in which diversity is still not sufficiently taken into account. Ruoyi and I don't see much of one another, but I watch with anticipation where her professional career will take her.

After my university years in Canterbury, I arrived in Brussels in September 2018 to begin a master's in International Conflict and Security, still with the University of Kent. I rented a tiny studio for myself on Rue de Pascale, just opposite Parc Leopold and very close to Parc du Cinquantenaire: green spaces are my touchstones in cities. I needed to be close to the earth and the trees in case things didn't go well. Greenness has always calmed me, it brings me home to the forests of Castellterçol, where through all four seasons of the year we can do 'forest bathing', a Japanese practice called *shinrin-yoku* which connects nature, mind and body: a minimalist exercise that places nature at its centre and brings the individual into harmony with the vibrations of nature as a regenerative element. Nature also has a 'pause effect', as Zygmunt Bauman says in his book *Born Liquid*: in a dissatisfied society, nature has a slowing and reflective effect that helps people to process the rapid changes in society.

In Brussels, my diary was immediately filled with activities, screenings of documentaries financed by the UN and conferences at the various seats of the European Parliament and international organisations: on sub-Saharan immigration to European coasts, or the prevention of conflict in Syria, Somalia, Colombia... I tried to fit in all the conferences, the readings for the master's seminars and a social life in my spare time but with little success. In spite of the general coldness of the people and the depressing effect the city had on me, it was satisfying to recognise the virtual perimeters of the 'European Union bubble', as the peculiar community that lived and worked around the European Union was called: more than forty thousand people from all continents. It was interesting to discover that so many citizens of the world were connected by a linguistic thread – English – and especially that we were creating a network of global knowledge. The city was full of Spaniards, Italians and French... all in search of job offers in sectors that were not well represented at home. Brussels would be a launch pad for many of us.

Despite being very sure that I wanted to do a master's in an international setting with people from different backgrounds, as with my undergraduate degree, I'd often be overcome by an immense, deep-rooted insecurity in my body that interfered with my plan to surround myself with ambitious people, those who vomit their CVs and their family background in your face at the first hello. Even though thanks to Ricard and Anna I'd achieved social and economic privileges and now belonged to the well-to-do European middle class, I'd grown up without truly owning them. The girl inside me, a girl who'd had nothing, was essentially unchanged.

My neighbour in the little flat in Rue de Pascale, a postgraduate student from Bogotá, had told me that winter in Brussels would have been very hard if he hadn't formed a network of friends in the city. Being an introvert, I didn't see it as such a big deal. I'd already mastered being alone. One of the benefits of leaving home at nineteen to study in England was that I'd learned to be happy in my own company: arriving in an unknown city and wandering around its museums and cinemas, and attending conferences. But as soon as the Belgian winter set in, anxiety took hold of me, and I wanted to run back to Barcelona, the city where winter never really comes; where Christmas Day appetisers with the family can be served outdoors: on the terrace of my grandmother's flat, which has views over all of Barcelona from the neighbourhood of El Guinardó to the Mediterranean in the distance or on the porch at home in Castellterçol, with views of the fields and forest. I was about to give it up. But I'd grown up believing I had to fulfil my commitments, and leaving the master's unfinished seemed like a whim and a squandering of too big a privilege. I was impatient, I wanted to grow quickly, have everything done already.

I survived the winter. Some of my master's class-mates – Jamie, Fee, Marie and Adheip – and I made a good team. We all came from very different parts of the world and there was a will to learn from each other; we understood each other very well, despite our different cultures and ambitions. Fee, who was from Amsterdam, and I prepared *injera* in a dinner we organised. We were like Brenda and Jasmin from *Bagdad Cafe*, a German comedy from 1987 directed by Percy Adlon, which always puts me in a very good mood. It was the first time I'd cooked *injera* from start to finish. On Sundays we'd meet up to watch films in Jamie's flat and end up listening to him play guitar while Adheip sang. An Englishman from Maidstone, the capital of the county of Kent where I'd done my degree, and an Indian from Bhubaneswar, the capital of the state of Odisha in eastern India. Two sensitive, creative, intelligent people. They all taught me so much. About innocence and the mistakes you make in your early twenties and the need to cultivate the mind for what keeps you restless. We were honest with each other, or perhaps not, but being together calmed us and that family feeling drove the meet-ups that followed in Barcelona, Amsterdam... Without a doubt, friendships like these were to be cherished.

However, Brussels could be a pleasant city too. It was delightful in the spring to sit with a book on a bench in Parc Leopold, a little paradise surrounded by offices and the headquarters of European institutions. Every weekend I'd go to the park with a book and some fruit, and stay there until it grew cool. It was one of the international hubs of the political world, along with Washington and Nairobi, and the rhythm of the city was suffocating, even though because of my Political Science studies I felt I was where I needed to be. What's more, at that time the subject of the Catalonian bid for independence was at its most imperative: it had been only a year since President Carles Puigdemont, Minister Toni Comín and other Catalan politicians had been in exile in Belgium and were lobbying the European Parliament. I wanted to understand the legal limits of the European Union to resolve a secession conflict within one of its member states, and the consequences of it turning its back on domestic 'political violence' inside the European Union, especially when Europe was aspiring to maintain its role of 'mentor' to Africa, Asia and the Americas. My final thesis was on this subject. It aspired to propose solutions, an alternative way that assumed the transformation of political culture to overcome the legal limits of the European Union. The 'Catalan case' wasn't only a challenge for Spain, but also placed the European Union in a critical position. In a way, Catalonia's political aspirations were possible thanks to the instruments of representation, at all levels, of the European Union, resulting from its project of political integration. Its silence put its credibility as an international institution at risk.

ʓ

The year 2018 was one that Ethiopians of my generation won't forget. It was a year of hope, and Ethiopia filled the headlines of international newspapers. My country of origin moved from headlines about poverty and drought to reports of it being one of the countries developing at a vertiginous rate. In a single year of leadership, Abiy Ahmed, the youngest prime minister in the history of Ethiopia (and the first Oromo to occupy the chief executive role), had promoted Ethiopia's role as mediator of conflicts in the Horn of Africa, following the example of former leaders such as Haile Selassie. It was also a year of return: Eritreans were able to go back to see their families in Ethiopia for the first time in twenty-five years and the Ethiopian opposition could also return, thanks to Abiy Ahmed's reconciliation policies. Ethiopia was making the transition from socialist politics with a protectionist economy to a liberal, democratic system, one with an economy that was open to outsiders and that attracted international powers intent on investing in the country's economic growth, such as the countries of the Persian Gulf.

In late May 2019, Abiy Ahmed wrote a letter to the children and young Ethiopians of the diaspora inviting them to take part in the transition. Even though this letter was part of a political strategy to grow the tourism sector and increase the nation's capital, it had symbolic meaning for me. The 'children of Ethiopia', including me, were invited to return and invest in our country of origin. In economic reform, the government had prioritised the diaspora. Abiy Ahmed was opening the doors to the new generations of Ethiopians who had inherited the political concerns and aspirations of their exiled or emigrant parents, or, as in my case, who had been adopted around the world. Perhaps it was the letter for which I'd waited so many years. I was one of those who burst into tears every time I left Ethiopia, knowing that it would be a while before I returned and many things would have changed, and I too would come back different, older. The letter was a symbol that validated my link to Ethiopia. It felt important to me that this letter would go to all the adopted Ethiopian boys and girls in the world (more than four thousand of whom were in Spain), not least to those who still hadn't found their identity. Because if we deserved one thing it was the freedom to choose where we belonged and how we defined ourselves.

7

For a long time, I was convinced that invisibility was the quality that most helped me to survive the early years of my life in Ethiopia. I continued to be largely invisible in Barcelona, Canterbury and Brussels. Until I met Dalil.

I saw Dalil for the first time as he was coming out of a master's seminar, at the end of the theories of conflict and violence class. As he gathered his things, and my classmates and I waited at the door to begin our class, he looked at me. I couldn't bear the intensity of his gaze and smiled. The idea of leaving Brussels without knowing who that young man was worried me. Someone told me his name and I decided to look him up on Facebook and send him a message. I easily discovered that he was half Ethiopian and half Algerian, an unusual genetic and cultural mix. A week later we met in Café Belge in Place Flagey to have a beer, although we began by talking about Ethiopian coffee.

He had delicate hands, wore impeccable clothes, had short curly hair and a smile. I was fascinated by his gestures, his passion and above all the obvious connection between us. We had enough family stories to fill a multivolume encyclopedia like those of old. There were only three years between us. He explained that he'd been born in Addis Ababa, where he had lived until the age of fourteen. The son of an Algerian diplomat and an Ethiopian model, he had grown up between two continents, Africa and Europe. Even though his adolescence had been shaped by the different places in which his parents worked, his maternal grandfather had had a great influence on his vision and interest in the politics and history of Ethiopia.

∩

I left Ethiopia at the age of seven, and at that time Ethiopian politics were very distant to me. From adolescence onwards I volunteered in different projects funded by AFNE (Association of Families of Ethiopian Children), founded in Barcelona in 2003 with the aims of helping with post-adoption issues, promoting Ethiopian culture and also of participating in projects related to child nutrition and preschool learning in rural Ethiopia. One of AFNE's ambitions was that those who had arrived as little ones would, once grown, assume the responsibility of helping each other to stay connected to their culture and country of origin. Despite my experience of humanitarian work in Ethiopia, my Eurocentric education seemed to limit my knowledge of the African world and trapped me in stereotypes or ideologies I didn't want to reproduce or impose. At heart, I still didn't believe that Ethiopian politics could change and become capable of generating prosperity for the majority of its citizens. It seemed absurd to focus my future professional life in Ethiopia when I'd managed to escape from my fate there. Who was I to reproduce the white saviour mentality? What was my role outside the privilege that had been granted to me by pure chance? What role should people like me play once we have adopted another culture, a new identity? In order to find answers to these questions, I knew that I had to distance myself physically from where my roots were: Ethiopia and Catalonia.

6bb

Between sips of Belgian beer, Dalil was showing me political maps of Ethiopia on the screen of his phone, illustrating the accounts of the Battle of Adwa in 1896, where the Ethiopians fought against and defeated the Italian army. This was to be the first Italo-Ethiopian war that Ethiopia managed to win against a European empire, against all odds. A battle that would be key to Ethiopia's national identity and to its position as the only non-colonised African country. This legacy can still be perceived in the geopolitical role Ethiopia plays on the continent and in the power dynamics of African institutions, strengthened by the alliances Ethiopia forged with imperial powers to expel Benito Mussolini's regime from the country. In 1936, the emperor of Ethiopia, Haile Selassie, would be the first African leader to speak at the League of Nations in Geneva, appealing to international values at the dawn of collective security. Twenty years later he delivered another speech, at the seat of the United Nations in New York, about the political will to achieve tangible change in the field of international security. He said: 'The goal of the equality of man which we seek is the antithesis of the exploitation of one people by another with which the pages of history, and in particular those written of the African and Asian continents, speak at such length.' A fact that many Western institutions forget, which could have major consequences for the future of relations between the European continent and the African one.

Dalil also spoke with pride of the constitution of the Organisation of African Unity in 1964 with its seat in Addis Ababa (which preceded the current African Union, founded in 2002) and of the independence of Eritrea in 1993 in a referendum backed by the UN after the end of the thirty-year war between Eritrea and Ethiopia. He spoke to me about the country's diversity, its different cultures, different identities, different languages and the difficulty of managing all this diversity with weak institutions. He spoke to me about poverty and about the country's natural riches and about its promising future under the leadership of Abiy Ahmed (this he said sceptically) – things that other Ethiopians of the diaspora had told me with pride. I could have listened to him for hours. I asked him how he would define his identity and he answered: 'I wear two hats and, according to the identity I choose at a particular time and in a particular context, I put on one or the other.'

The subject of identity has been a key element in my integration into Catalonia and into Europe generally. Identity is formed by internal elements, such as the will to define yourself, and external elements, according to how you are recognised by the society in which you live. I was ready to question it all. From Dalil I learned that a dual identity is a tool that enriches you as a person. We were quite different: he had a self-esteem that I lacked, and I was keen to widen my outlook. I believed that intolerance could only be combated by travel, by connecting with people with different experiences. Beneath our shared need to demonstrate our knowledge about our political centres (Catalonia, Algeria, Ethiopia), his vulnerability drew my attention. In his nostalgia, and for the first time in years, I felt understood. Dalil saw me.

ჸ

In Zygmunt Bauman's book *Retrotopia*, I underlined a quote by Svetlana Boym, professor of Slavic and Comparative Literatures at Harvard University: 'Nostalgia is a sentiment of loss and displacement, but it is also a romance with one's own fantasy. […] The twentieth century began with a futuristic utopia and ended with nostalgia. […] There is a global epidemic of nostalgia, an affective yearning for a community with a collective memory, a longing for continuity in a fragmented world. […] The danger of nostalgia is that it tends to confuse the actual home and the imaginary one.'

ჸ

As it grew dark and Café Belge filled with people, Dalil and I moved from Ethiopian to Catalan politics, family and childhood, as if we'd known each other all our lives. He promised me a good *bunna* at his home and we left it there.

THE TURQUOISE
DOOR OF GONDAR

One morning I went to see Yamrot in that room which terrified me so much, full of sick women cared for by the Calcutta missionaries. It was a room with rows of beds, set out in such a way that there was a central aisle. Yamrot was almost indistinguishable among so many equally sick women. She'd lost so much weight it was hard for me to see the Yamrot with the energy and character I knew. I went over and held her hand until in a weak voice she sent me to Mikaele. Now more than ever I was in charge of my little brother, she told me.

The next day I went back to see Yamrot, following the routine of that centre which had enveloped me in its warmth, that centre which already seemed like it could be our new home. I jumped up the steps thinking about how it would be if the three of us lived there; with Yamrot's skills she'd find a way of making a place for herself, in the kitchen or taking care of children, as the other women did, of that I was sure. But Yamrot wasn't in her bed. A nun in the immaculate white sari came running after me. I understood immediately what had happened and sat down on the steps in front of the infirmary with my head between my legs, crying uncontrollably, repeating a single word: 'Nanney, Nanney…' Again and again, as if I were mid-prayer. Nanney was the diminutive I used to address Yamrot. Nanney was also the word with which I begged forgiveness when she hit me with a strap if I'd done something bad. They didn't let me see her dead. It was 16 March 2003.

I was seven and Mikaele three when we became orphans in the Missionaries of Charity centre in Gondar. It seemed deliberate. As if Yamrot had somehow gone to die in the best possible place at that time, in the safest place. Since leaving Ethiopia I've wondered again and again how I had the luck to end up in Sister Mariska's hands. Because she and the other women in that centre saved me, saved my future.

The last time I saw Mikaele he was dead, in his bed. Then they made me leave and they closed the two doors that gave access to the children's infirmary, one from the bedroom where I slept and the other from the garden. And later I watched how the nuns took his lifeless body away, covered with a white sheet, to the communal pit of Gondar cemetery. Where they'd also buried Yamrot. It was 27 March 2003.

θ

Later on, when a few African countries and the entire Mediterranean separated me from Ethiopia, I'd learn that Yamrot had had Aids. According to the World Health Organisation, in 2003 Ethiopia was one of the countries most affected by Aids. Around two million people lived with HIV, which had first been detected in the mid-1980s. Since then infections had hugely affected both the rural and urban populations. That year, more than 120,000 people (both adults and children) died from Aids in Ethiopia. Yamrot was one of them, and Mikaele was another. In a country with such unreliable statistic-gathering, I wonder whether there weren't many more people that no one counted. Untreated children infected by mother-to-child transmission usually lived to around the age of two; only a third would live to the age of five. In 2003 I would be one of the 720,000 boys and girls orphaned because of Aids. The data are also clear on the fact that young women were the most affected by the disease.

Beating Aids is one of the biggest challenges for global development in Ethiopia. Aids is synonymous with loss of life and loss of productivity, with the economy suffering at both an individual and collective level. Looking at graphs charting the frequency of HIV infections is shocking. Like all development indicators, the mortality rate from Aids has fallen, especially since 2008, when the number of new infections plateaued. According to information from UNAIDS (the joint United Nations programme on HIV/Aids), this positive progress is due to the increased and improved resources for dealing with the disease, and above all to the inclusion of Aids on the national agenda. The public health response is joined by the improvement and strengthening of the system of government, and the coordinated promotion of human rights and gender equality.

The lowest levels of government in Ethiopia, delivered by what are called *kebeles*, are in charge of implementing awareness and education programmes, but tensions between national government and local government hamper sustained progress. The majority of Aids-infected people live in the countryside, where there is less access to information about the disease and greater difficulty in accessing health services. Improving the standard of living of people with Aids is an economic problem. Reducing the number of deaths means reducing the economic instability within a family and within the community. Over the last twenty years, in terms of Aids, the gap between the rural and urban worlds has become even more evident.

An article published in *Plus Medicine* in 2020 on the efficiency of culturally appropriate interventions to prevent gender violence and the transmission of Aids between men and women in rural Ethiopia concluded that the areas most affected by Aids were those where levels of domestic violence were highest. In Ethiopia, the prevalence of physical and sexual violence against women within a couple (heterosexual, because homosexuality was still forbidden under penalty of imprisonment) was more than 70 per cent.

Where life is precarious, rates of sexually transmitted illness and sexual violence are highest. I had survived both, against the odds.

6.

As soon as Mikaele died, I became very sick. My immune system collapsed at once, sounding the alarm. The nuns, accustomed to seeing how the processes of grief and trauma manifested themselves, watched as little by little I stopped eating: my tonsils were totally inflamed. One morning, they lifted me out of bed and found the lymph nodes under my arms completely swollen too. Tonsillitis stopped me swallowing anything, or even talking, and I couldn't move my arms because of the swollen glands. Sister Mariska and a carer called Bisrat lifted me into a blue Gondar taxi, and all three of us crossed the little eucalyptus wood just behind the Calcutta missionaries' centre, until we stopped in front of a house with a garden surrounded by a stone wall. It had been many days since I'd gone beyond the centre's turquoise metallic door. Or perhaps not so many. For me time was always difficult to measure.

An old man who knew Sister Mariska came out to welcome us, dressed in a thick white *netela* and plastic sandals. They immediately placed two chairs in the garden, one in front of the other. The man went back into the house and came out with a round metal tray, painted with red flowers on a white background, like the ones normally used for collecting coffee cups. But this one was full of surgical instruments and leaves and stems of the plant used in the coffee ceremony. He placed it on the ground and made me sit on one chair while he sat on the one in front. He threw the green stalks at my feet and he placed leaves on my head. I didn't understand what this man was doing, I didn't know whether the leaves were what would cure me, or the terrifying collection of needles and knives on the tray. If he wanted me to keep my head upright, I already knew how to do it perfectly well without their tricks. In Dansha I'd often accompanied Yamrot and our neighbours and their children to wash clothes in the river. On the way back, when we'd bathed and the clothes had been draped over bushes to dry, we would all carry a bucket of water on our heads and our already-dry clothes tied to our backs. Keeping your head upright while carrying something important like water was something I already knew how to do.

Once I was seated and still, Sister Mariska and Bisrat suddenly pinned me hard to the chair while the man opened my mouth and, with a very quick movement, pulled out my tonsils with some tweezers. Just like that, without preamble, without any kind of anaesthetic. Tears fell from my eyes from the pressure the tweezers made and the locking of my jaw. I gave in.

After I recovered from that episode, Sister Mariska subjected me to a regime of injections, morning and afternoon, until little by little I began to regain my strength and a sense of curiosity about where I was living and what was going on. I was sick of the white rice two missionaries made me eat every day. I was on the brink of malnutrition and they were doing their best to rehabilitate me. I wasn't the first little girl who had lived in these conditions, and I wouldn't be the last. Day after day many people at the end of their means would come, and, if they could, the missionaries would always prioritise the women and children. In fact, many sick women with little children who had nothing, as in Yamrot's case, would try to reach the Missionaries of Charity centre when they realised they might soon die. Because if a woman died inside there, on the other side of the turquoise door, their orphaned children would be looked after by the missionaries and never be returned to the street unprotected and alone.

T

I still have gaps of information and I believe I'll always want to fill them. I want to fill them for myself, but also for those who perhaps still ask each other what became of Yamrot and her children. I want to believe that Yamrot's name is still brought up in family conversations during the coffee ceremony; or in the kitchen, while the *injera* dough is being prepared; or when they're chatting while sifting small stones from lentils. I like to imagine that Yamrot has never left the thoughts of those who knew her, and even that she is a thought that they don't dare speak aloud at a celebration: whether it be a birth, a wedding or a burial, she is there. Many years have passed and I am the continuation of Yamrot's story, and I refuse to accept Yamrot as a mere number, just one of the many women driven from their place of origin, disappeared women or female victims of poverty in the statistics of an international organisation studying Ethiopia with a magnifying glass.

Yamrot *was* a victim of structural Ethiopian poverty, but she was much more than that. She was a young woman with dreams, courage and plenty of drive but very few resources. They tell me I'm resilient, but she was even more so. Yamrot is my past, but also my present. I want to believe I've inherited her perseverance as well as her unmistakeable genes,

which link me to all the Ethiopian women with
their roots in the countryside, in the mountains of
the Amhara region to the Simien and beyond. The
still visible scars on my skin are receptacles of my
childhood memories. They say that with my *nikisat*,
the tattoo Yamrot carved on my forehead when I was
a very little girl, I can only be from a village, because
it hasn't been done on city girls for decades. It gives
me enormous pride: my heart is in the countryside,
in the mountains. Even though my nails aren't dirty
from working the land and my hands aren't wrinkled
and chapped from gathering damp eucalyptus wood,
I carry with me all the marks and signs of a woman
who has lived in the green mountains and dense
forests of northern Ethiopia.

U

Three years after the deaths of Yamrot and Mikaele,
the moment came to revisit the same roads I had
travelled with them, from Wereta to Humera, but
now accompanied by Ricard and Anna. Throughout
the journey in a jeep, covering many kilometres over
difficult roads and dirt tracks, sleeping and eating in
very modest, poor places, beginning in Addis Ababa
and ending in the last city before the border with
Eritrea, my parents and I were seeing fragments of my
first childhood. We were visiting the places I'd told

them about with so much delight during the three years I'd lived with them.

At every street corner there was a reflection of us: Yamrot, Mikaele and me. And also a little of Getachew, my elder brother. The deeper we went into the Amhara region towards Tigray, the more of my roots appeared. Women and girls with tattooed foreheads like mine, with suns or Orthodox crosses, others with patterns tattooed on their necks or arms. Elegant women dressed in simple flowered dresses, gathered at the waist, like the one I'd had, watched us from the doors of their homes, which had adobe walls and roofs made from asbestos and tree branches, their children clutching their hands or at their breasts, or sitting on stools combing or braiding each other's hair. To their eyes we must have seemed a strange combination, even though many would have worked out what was going on: I was an orphaned girl with *farangi* parents.

I was focused on understanding how my destiny had turned upside down in such a short time. I was coming back to my country of origin for the first time without understanding the language. My Amharic had been wiped out completely. I was coming back without an Ethiopian family to root me. I was ten in 2006, and although still a little girl, I realised that not only had I lost my family but that my identity, my culture and my language of origin had been stripped from me too. In Europe, and around wealthy Africans, I couldn't explain how unjust this seemed to me. In the eyes of everyone who was curious about my family background I was a very privileged girl who had been saved. I was furious. I think now I was angry with everyone and with my country. Neither my mother nor my family had abandoned me. Ethiopia had abandoned me. Like so many children, and other forgotten sectors of society, we were products of a global economic system that generated inequalities and territorial imbalances. Behind the rage, there's always been the simple need to explain what had become of me, who I had become far from the Wereta mountains. I wanted to explain that I was ready to use the privilege that had come to me unasked, maybe undeserved; that I was ready to turn it into a good tool, to propel me to become everything Yamrot had wanted for us.

ለ

I returned to Gondar one rainy July morning in 2006, and I knocked at the turquoise metallic door of the missionaries, followers of Teresa of Calcutta. This time I was prepared for what awaited me behind it. I was nervous. I'd been crying for days. Of all the trips back I've taken so far, that first one in 2006 was the one on which I cried the most. I cried all the tears

I hadn't cried in the three years in Catalonia, where I'd thrown myself into learning so many things and getting maximum enjoyment from the full, happy childhood my new parents had offered me. The wave of feelings and emotions was strong. I felt rage and a lot of sorrow. In only three years away from my country, I'd already changed and so had my perspective and standard of living. That place which to me had seemed a refuge among rose bushes, idyllic at times, was now a decaying welcome centre for very sick people who could barely stand up straight. It was the place where I'd seen the two people who were my whole world die. But this time I was going back to show it to Ricard and Anna, to seek information and, above all, to be able to thank Sister Mariska for all she had done to help us.

On seeing us, Sister Mariska became very emotional. Since she had become director of the centre in Gondar, some years before, no one had ever come back to say thank you or to look for information about their origins. In fact, two of us girls were the first to come back with our new families: Banchi and I, who were the same age. I'd met Banchi in 2004, when she came as an adoptee to Barcelona a short time after me. We would see each other from time to time, and from our chats, when Banchi could speak Catalan fluently, we discovered that we'd lived almost in the same towns in northern Ethiopia and been welcomed by the same missionaries, but not at the same time. I had left Gondar before she arrived with her sick mother. It wasn't the first coincidence to happen to me. In August 2003, leaving the consulting room of the paediatrician and specialist in tropical medicine Doctor Vicky Fumadó, in the Sant Joan de Déu Hospital in Barcelona, I came face to face with Sintayehu. He was a boy I'd met in the missionary centre in Addis Ababa, where I lived for barely four months after the stay in the centre in Gondar. I think we even gave a bounce and a little shout from the surprise. Sintayehu and I burst out laughing and stared at each other, almost like two adults doing wordless inspections, while our parents looked on, impressed by the scene two children were making in that hospital waiting room. Sintayehu had left the Addis Ababa orphanage before me and I remembered perfectly the moment a *farangi* had taken him away in a taxi parked in the yard. But of course I didn't know where he had gone and didn't at all expect to see him coming out the door of that consulting room.

When Banchi and I discovered so many coincidences between our experiences, our parents decided that the two families should travel to Ethiopia together during the summer holidays. I wasn't excited at all, not even a little bit: I knew I'd have to face some hard memories. I wondered what would happen if someone recognised me and claimed me, something that didn't seem at all far-fetched. At the end of the day, I was nothing more than a package. In any case, I didn't have a choice. Anna and Ricard didn't let me choose: we would go and that was that. And I'll always be thankful.

Banchi wanted to try to find her older brother. And she did. In Dansha. Their reunion was an intense moment and made me think of Getachew. I've looked for him on Facebook, as others have done with greater success. I've also seen many Ethiopians looking for their children who were adopted in Catalonia and other parts of Europe when they could have taken care of them. Abiy Ahmed's government stopped international adoptions expressly to reduce the number of children adopted by mistake (or through unapproved international organisations, or trafficked). I've looked for Getachew everywhere, but I still haven't found him. Sister Mariska showed us the file where they kept all the information about the children who had passed through their centre in Gondar. We found the sheet where they had written down my answers the day we arrived with the policemen: Yamrot's name, Mikaele's name, my name, our ages, where we were coming from, where we were going. And a colour photograph of Mikaele and me, holding hands, stuck to the same page. They took it just after Yamrot's death, when we became orphans; and a very few days before he died; before Sister Mariska and the other nuns said goodbye to me and made me get into a car driven by a stranger, sitting on the back seat with a missionary I'd never seen before who carried a well-wrapped baby on her lap.

It was 28 April 2003. Sister Mariska had taken the trouble to find my sheet in the file and add that information to it. We travelled throughout the day, which felt never-ending to me, on roads in a very bad state, one jolt after another, leaving dead Yamrot and Mikaele behind. I remember sleeping with my head against the legs of the woman, whose name I didn't even know, and that I was woken by the constant juddering of the car.

We stopped at another little missionary centre in Debre Markos before reaching Addis Ababa, more than six hundred kilometres south of Gondar, at nightfall. There the missionaries had a much bigger welcome centre for sick people. And also a little orphanage where the healthier boys and girls were kept, and the staff tried to find them adoptive families around the world, through international adoption agencies.

h

Yamrot had migrated to the north of the country for economic reasons, seeking work. From Wereta to Gondar and from there to Dansha and finally to

Humera. The journey from Humera to Gondar was the last that I completed with Yamrot, as we made our way back to Wereta. If someone had claimed me then, they might have sent me to Wereta and perhaps I could have lived with my uncle and aunt. But without Yamrot I was nobody. In barely four months I went from being undocumented in my own country to becoming a Catalan citizen with a Spanish passport, a European with full rights. I was issued an official birth certificate in 2003, seven years after my birth, by the Spanish embassy in Addis Ababa, so that I could obtain a passport. I'd never celebrated a birthday and I didn't know when I'd been born, so Ricard and Anna decided to put down the day we'd met in the yard of the Missionaries of Charity centre in Addis Ababa and subtract seven years. Well, five years, in fact. The missionaries lied about my age when I was put up for international adoption and took two years off the age I'd told them on arrival at their centre in Gondar, thinking it would be easier to find me a family that way. They were aware that most adoptive families around the world want boys and girls as young as possible. The younger the children, the weaker their family and cultural ties are.

Ricard and Anna always say that when they met me it was clear to them that I wasn't five years old as they'd been told. Although I was very small and weighed very little, my expression, my way of speaking and the quantity of memories I described couldn't be those of a five-year-old. When we got to Barcelona a huge number of medical tests were done on me. The X-rays of the bones in my wrist and my teeth, among others, conclusively showed that I'd been born in 1996, so was already seven years old. After we received the news, all of us together in Dr Vicky Fumadó's consulting room, I called every member of my new family (grandmother, grandfather, my new elder siblings through Ricard…) from the car on the way home, amused. And to everyone I repeated the same phrase in Catalan I'd learned by heart, because I was still mixing Amharic with my first words of Catalan: 'Hello, I'm seven, not five!' But there would be two fewer years on my passport and birth certificate for a long time…

The story of my gender would be even longer. A civil servant from the Spanish embassy in Addis Ababa (I'm convinced it was a man) saw my passport photo, with my head completely shaved because of ringworm and lice, and my abbreviated name, which in Amharic could be male or female, and decided that I was a boy, without even thinking to check, and calmly registered me as male on my birth certificate as well as on my passport. Luckily, when we came to collect the passport at the embassy, Anna and Ricard noticed the mistake, and it was corrected then and there. But my birth certificate had already been sent to the Central Civil Register in Madrid. The odyssey of correcting the year of birth and putting my gender as female involved years of procedures in Barcelona and Madrid, and a lot of bureaucracy, medical tests, money and patience. This continued until I visited a female forensic doctor on the Civil Register in Plaça Medinaceli in Barcelona, who had ploughed through the weighty file of tests and documents. When she saw me come through the door, well into adolescence, she didn't even ask me to take off my jacket. There was a hearing at the Ciutat de la Justícia in L'Hospitalet de Llobregat. And the verdict was in my favour: I was a woman and born in 1996.

◌◌

Yamrot was twenty-five when she died. Writing this at the same age now as she was then, I have a future full of possibilities. What is for me the beginning of adult life was the end for her. And this is unfair. Especially since there are millions of women in Ethiopia living in conditions similar to those in which she lived. Those in which I lived as a little girl. Many wealthy, urban Ethiopians don't like you talking about the poverty of their country. It's a subject that hasn't been resolved and has been used too many times by international agencies to undermine the country's sovereignty. But I can talk about extreme poverty first-hand and directly, because it was my reality during the seven years I lived in Ethiopia. Until the last boy and girl on earth can enjoy a good-quality education and a secure, protected childhood, we must talk about it as much as we can. My country of origin is very rich culturally, and in natural resources, but it needs huge investment in its people. Investing in young people and in the education of women is crucial for the prosperity of any country.

ሠ

The psychological effect of poverty is something that hasn't been explored enough. How long does it take to escape the guilt of coming from a society that lives in a constant state of precariousness? How long does it take you to raise your head and look people in the eyes, knowing that it is possible to give yourself strength and possible to speak up about instability, about the political powers' disregard for citizens, children's education and the endemic violence against women?

ረ

The economy, the development of rural life and the possibility of creating opportunities in villages and small cities are things that must be at the core of the political debate in any state. A democratic society is usually created by expanding the middle class and reducing poverty. How can a government be aware of enormous poverty and not conclude that, if the will were there, all those people could be productive and could contribute to the country's growth?

'Many live in poverty and are consumed each day by dealing with existential basics of hunger, cold and a constant threat of violence. When life involves so much effort not to get hurt, demoralised or damaged, it's easy to believe society's message that those who aren't thriving are themselves at fault,' wrote Sophie Walker in her book *Five Rules for Rebellion: Let's Change the World Ourselves*. It's about will and it's about power. Having more than one hundred and twenty million inhabitants makes Ethiopia a state that is difficult to manage, but that shouldn't be a reason to neglect those in the countryside, nor to allow families who find themselves outside the nuclei of opportunities to be abandoned to their fate. The Ethiopian government must reclaim those spaces previously occupied by humanitarian actors. This can be done by creating workplaces and local organisations that promote social care. Because it's about many people, millions of people.

No one in Yamrot's condition should be rescued from the other side of a turquoise metallic door.

DECULTURALISATION

I met Dalil again two years later, once more in Brussels, in the autumn of 2020. I'd spent a year working with the Horn of Africa team of political analysts from the International Crisis Group think tank (half the year physically in Kenya and the other half working remotely, repatriated due to Covid-19). We met for dinner at a restaurant in Place Jourdan and as soon as we took our seats, it felt as though we'd seen each other the day before. We were still the same, but our views on Ethiopian politics had matured. We felt like the students in the 1970s who came back to Ethiopia to turn politics upside down. Ethiopians of our generation weren't so different: we too aspired to turn the country upside down, on an economic and digital level, where today's revolutions take place. Like many researchers, we foresaw that there would be a war: tensions were so high that the country was barely functioning day-to-day. We wondered whether there could be another kind of politics, one that banished the cycles of violence, the corruption and the partisanship and focused on the rural population, which was still mired in poverty. From time to time, Dalil and I would comment on articles via Twitter, in a kind of intermittent private debate. In one message he told me that the rural population, which formed 80 per cent of the Ethiopian population, was the future of Ethiopia. The issue was not a lack of wealth: Ethiopia and the whole African continent are very rich. The issue was how to introduce development and improve quality of life around the country without leaving anyone behind.

The Renaissance Dam, formerly known as the Millennium Dam, is now called the GERD (Grand Ethiopian Renaissance Dam). The construction of this dam began in 2011 to store the water of the Blue Nile – the source of which is in Ethiopia – and to solve the country's electricity problems. It was to be a catalyst of change for the women and girls who had to go to fetch water and wood in dangerous conditions, and who were, as a result, deprived of the chance to continue their studies. Talking all this over with Dalil, I saw the frustration in his heavy-handed arguments; he was projecting his disappointment onto our conversation. But we returned to anecdotes from our childhoods and looked to the future in order to escape from reality. Fate had brought us back to the same place, Brussels, and I wondered what he would teach me this time.

Thanks to conversations with Dalil I began to see my country of origin with fresh eyes. I'd gone back six times in seventeen years. They were stays of different kinds that helped me acquire a pretty good understanding of Ethiopia and its diversity, from the thousands of kilometres which connect Danakil Depression, one of the hottest places on earth, where those from Afar would collect blocks of salt, to the rock-hewn Orthodox churches of Lalibela, to the churches on the little islands in the middle of Lake Tana; stopping to listen to stories about the age of princes in the memorable castles of Gondar; to the emblematic door of Harar, which opens out to the Muslim world. I persisted in saying that I felt abandoned by my country of birth. I knew it had failed many of us and would continue to fail many more if the equitable distribution of resources wasn't prioritised, if political conflicts weren't resolved peacefully, and if technological instruments to streamline the processes of economic development weren't integrated. I blamed it for the perennial structural inequality which sealed the fate of my mother, Yamrot, and continued to shape the destinies of many women like her, and of many girls and future women like me.

Dalil and I come from radically different Ethiopian social classes: he is part of the privileged Ethiopian elite and I come from the 'invisible masses', 'the 80 per cent', the poorest sector of Ethiopia. And because

of that, I saw from the first minute that our experiences and sometimes our opinions on what feminism,
politics and development mean in Ethiopia were
different; I had a feeling of hopelessness that tainted
my arguments. But we did agree on one key idea: if
I had grown up in Ethiopia, I wouldn't have become
the woman I am today, which to a large extent is due
to my adoptive parents. The initial fight for my future
was made by Yamrot. Anna and Ricard continued it.

Identity is a constant process of definition and construction. As the young Catalan and European I felt
myself to be, I realised that, without understanding
the historical context of thousands of women who live
in rural Ethiopia, I would never come to understand
my origins, or make peace with the Ethiopian state.
And with this thought I began what seemed to be
a second search for my origins, one that focused on
exploring the political, social and economic contexts
in which Yamrot lived, in which I was born. I have
no biological family in Ethiopia (if I do, I don't know
how to find it, or maybe I haven't searched widely
enough); I have no contact with anyone who might
have known Yamrot. My story was destined to be the
same as that of all those women who are part of this
rural 80 per cent, with high rates of illiteracy and poverty. And in this sense, I believe that it's very powerful
to be able to position individual experience in the
context of collective experience. Perhaps that was

my problem: not having understood that a discourse on identity must be contextualised within the social changes in which one's own journey began. And to understand at last that coming from a poor family can be a tool to combat global structural inequality. A tool to fight against paternalism.

Because of that, although he was theoretically aware of poverty in Ethiopia, Dalil focused on the country's potential, and what it could have if it left violence behind, if it encouraged the education of young people and the creation of jobs instead of cultivating toxic patriotism. We both believed the country's political culture needed to change to end the collective generational trauma.

ሰ

Sometimes I think that the Catalan poet Maria-Mercè Marçal wrote her famous 'Divisa' with me in mind: 'I'm grateful to fate for three gifts: to have been born a woman, from the working class and an oppressed nation. And the turbid azure of being three times a rebel.'

ñ

In the process of defining my identity, the meeting points of the Ethiopian diaspora have helped me.

All the Ethiopian restaurants around the world, from Europe to Australia, have given me little windows into Ethiopian culture, many with background music of Ethiopian jazz fused with European music and the blues. And always scented with the aroma of freshly roasted coffee beans, transporting me to their origin, where roasting coffee is a daily activity, a long one, full of codes, and one that outside Ethiopia is an art in itself. I'd eagerly seek out these meeting points to be able to understand the Ethiopian diaspora and how it works. And to make the meeting points mine.

Washington state has the highest Ethiopian population outside Ethiopia and therefore in the United States. In Europe, the countries with the highest Ethiopian populations are Germany and the Netherlands. In 2018, according to Catalonia's Statistics Institute, 1,163 individuals adopted from Ethiopia were living in Catalonia; and only 107 adult Ethiopians were registered as foreign nationals.

Catalonia isn't a usual destination for Ethiopians because it doesn't have a flourishing network of immigrants from the country. The immigrant networks serve to create jobs for new arrivals and act as a link with the local community. But the most interesting thing is that they also help to preserve dual identity. I believe that this link between people who have been adopted and the immigrant community isn't discussed enough. The fact is that, independently of how we have arrived, what unites us is our origin and destination and the need to keep our dual identity: Ethiopian and Catalan (in whichever order you like).

In both adoptive and immigrant communities, we feel under pressure to forfeit our culture of origin in exchange for pure, immediate integration. For immigrants, cultural assimilation is a slow process. Whereas for us adopted people, this process is vertiginously quick, since not having a social network to foster and keep alive our original culture and language makes us lose them.

Boys who are adopted (curiously, it's more common among boys than girls) have a kind of 'second social integration test' on coming of age. A friend of mine of Ethiopian origin, whose adoptive parents had even changed his name to a very Catalan one, was stopped by a police officer one night on his way back from taking out the rubbish in the middle of Barcelona. They asked what he was doing in the street so late and demanded his identity card. He wasn't stopped because he'd thrown glass into the plastics container; no. He was clearly stopped because of the colour of his skin and because he might have been an undocumented African immigrant. Pure racism and prejudice.

The most racist treatment I've received was in Cuba. It was 2016. Ricard, Anna and I were coming back from dinner, and on entering our hotel in

Havana's old town, the nightwatchman (a white man) told us I couldn't come in. Instead of asking who I was or requesting my passport, which when in doubt would have been the correct thing to do, he assumed that I was a young prostitute who was going up to some tourist's room and blocked my way. My parents became very angry. The following morning the management of the hotel offered their apologies.

φ

Leaving to do my degree in England allowed me to meet many young people who were second-generation immigrants from different countries, and who taught me that origins remain resilient against the dominance of the adoptive culture. However, Blackness is a more difficult thing to maintain in a white family, especially in a society that has difficulties in passing on the culture, history and collective experience of Black people in the West. Catalonia's population, unlike other parts of Europe, isn't at all diverse. When I'm asked about racism, I answer that you should shift your point of reference in the world and turn the map upside down, because that's how racism is understood and eliminated from your vocabulary and therefore from your thoughts.

My university friend Omalade, who came to England from Nigeria with her parents when she was a little girl, introduced me fully to Black culture. She was a young woman who refused to change her identity no matter how much her environment reinforced the hostility or dissociation which means feeling or being a certain way, or being the way the majority want you to be. She gave me Maya Angelou's book *I Know Why the Caged Bird Sings*, which struck me as a great metaphor: my ideal world free of racism, free of prejudice, free of problems, which in essence was an image of a privileged reality. I started comparing my experience to Omalade's. She would snort with laughter at my ignorance about the world of Afro hair, the variety of African cuisine, African culture in general. We didn't have the same lived perceptions regarding Africans' colonial experience either: Ethiopians' inherent pride comes from the country's resistance to those very colonial forces; Nigerians can't feel the same way. In short, international adoption has, for me, become a prism, a lens that helps me to understand the world, the structural inequalities in immigration processes, social integration, the search for belonging, how the identity of a person is formed far from their roots...

Adoption seen through the frame of abandonment doesn't reflect my experience nor that of many others who were enriched until almost the end of our childhoods by a social environment – Ethiopian in my case – that was important and taught us vital lessons. For many, these childhood experiences have shaped our professional aspirations, and indeed have determined the kind of people we are and the family we want.

∩

When I first went back to Ethiopia, at the age of ten, I didn't want to know anything about my biological family. I had rejected Alamnew before leaving Ethiopia. And I certainly wouldn't have forgiven Yamrot if she'd left me with him. However, for me, enjoying the life I have now seems like a selfish act when I think of Getachew. Thinking about him hurts. What kind of life will he be living? Where?

Uprooting, and the forming of my identity far from my homeland, was a battle I wasn't prepared to lose. Deculturalisation is a little-explored process in adoption, as is the loss of elements necessary for forming identity. Very few adoptive parents have the energy to resolve the contradictions of educating a son or daughter who speaks a language they don't understand, because a world separates them. Today, when I discuss immigration, adoption and integration I equate the experience of Omalade – who can be considered a second-generation immigrant in England – with mine. This might make a large part of the adopted collective uncomfortable, above all those who have ended up in an extremely protective environment and have lost contact with their roots. I would argue that being economically affluent has made it easier for some adoptees to overlook racism and identity issues, as though they were subjects that have nothing to do with them, that don't apply to them.

Charlotte, a Vietnamese woman of my age, adopted by a French family when she was a baby, was my neighbour in the shared flat on Brussels' Chaussée de Wavre that I moved into in September 2020. She said I arrived in Europe when I was quite big and our two realities were very different. She had no links with Vietnam, or any desire to go back to it. Charlotte knew other Vietnamese-French women like her who had only gone back to visit their country of origin during adolescence because they were having problems at home or at school. For both Charlotte (with her Vietnamese appearance) and me (with my Ethiopian appearance), regardless of our European passports, prevailing racism means we're seen, at first glance, as immigrants, as 'outsiders'. I'm amazed that anyone can take shelter in their privilege when a whole community is affected by an oppressive system that doesn't differentiate, however much you have given up your racial and cultural identity. Everyone chooses their battles, but some are imposed on you, and for me racism is one of them.

Understanding identity in absolute terms is dangerous. It makes you turn your back on realities that must be changed altogether, not only when they affect you. It makes you believe that verbal racism is never intentional: it stems from good intentions, or from ignorance. The rise of the extreme right in Europe is a danger to migrants, and also a danger to all of us who are physiognomically different from the prevailing white majority. When I move through the world, it doesn't bother me that before anything else they look at my 'packaging'. I am European, I am African. But I don't want to have to worry anywhere about my physical safety on account of the colour of my skin, and even less so at home, in Catalonia.

My Barcelonian friend Yeshi, also adopted in Ethiopia at the same age as me, was sacked after two weeks by the bar where she was working, without being paid anything, with the excuse that they hadn't given her a contract. She didn't know whether she'd experienced a racist act or not. Until then she'd never thought that maybe she'd have to be prepared to confront this topic. Because she is and feels Catalan and that is enough. Not knowing whether people are racist towards her disorientates her. And embarrasses her. It makes me think about our privilege and about the suffering of those who have no passport, no documents to protect them.

✟

I have feminist parents who have educated me in feminist values. Often at home they've talked to me about the pay gap between men and women, about the importance of always wearing the 'gender lens' to be able to recognise and address gender inequalities in every field. Recently, over dinner, Anna told me that only about 20 per cent of companies in Catalonia are led by a woman. Having founded her company at the age of twenty-four, she was invited to become a member of the Board of Advisers for the Women, Business and Economy Observatory of Barcelona's Chamber of Commerce. That's amazing, I tell her. But how many women of African, Latin American or Asian origin are on this board? Not one. From my point of view it was clear that not finding them meant not looking hard enough. It is true that Catalonia became a destination for international immigration at the end of the 1980s and beginning of the 1990s, but it is still a long way from achieving the cultural and racial diversity across all social classes that exists in other parts of Europe. Perhaps it's true that there hasn't been enough time to create significant opportunities for businesswomen from ethnic minorities. But it's difficult for me to end all conversations about diversity this way, like the snake eating its own tail: there are none, and because there are none, we don't have any, and we don't have any because there are none. To correct structures of power, everything must be turned upside down, because at the end of the day it's about power.

The glass ceiling of which white European feminists speak so much is much more difficult for women of colour or immigrants to break. And going further, for the LGBTQI+ community too. The fight to have more women in decision-making roles is very important and still hasn't ended, not by a long shot. But alongside that, it's necessary to fight to normalise cultural and racial diversity and to make it visible. The key question was formulated quite a while ago by the African American politician and activist Angela Davis, and she repeated it at a wonderful conference at the University of Costa Rica in 2018: 'How is it that we could have ever thought it might be possible to achieve women's liberation while leaving behind Indigenous women, Latina women, Muslim women, Asian American women? [...] The most vibrant forms of feminism today are not what we once called "mainstream white bourgeois feminism".'

𝍢

You may have been born in London to parents from Ghana or Pakistan and always have been exposed to and embraced by your ancestral culture. That wasn't so for me. In my home, I was the ambassador of Ethiopian culture: music, language, food... I was my own link to Ethiopia and I was always my own 'cultural nucleus' in my new place.

I've talked with Dalil a lot about this subject because he too is part of this group of people who have dual or multiple identities. He is Ethiopian and Algerian but he is very European at the same time as being very African. We've spent hours trying to answer the question: 'What does it mean to be Ethiopian outside Ethiopia?' We agree on concerns about the country's current trajectory and how we can use our privilege to contribute from the outside to Ethiopia's social and political change. I find this kind of conversation very enriching because I've always wanted to understand my country of origin better and some day be of use to it. Many of us adoptees understand that if we are living in Europe as Europeans it is because at 'home' there are many things to improve. I don't like the idea of wanting to 'save' a country, but I do want to contribute as much as I can to improving the standard of living of its inhabitants.

In her book *Sensuous Knowledge: A Black Feminist Approach for Everyone*, Minna Salami dedicates an entire chapter to discussing identity. My whole book is underlined. Among many underlined paragraphs is this one: 'Rather than viewing identity as a weapon, we should view it as a compass. Like a compass, it helps guide the focus and direction in life. Your woman-compass can help you find distance from men who view women as inferior (if men are your thing). [...] Your black-compass prepares you when an institution you are working with has a legacy of racism. Your class-compass prevents you from feeling shame when you don't have access to the things financially privileged people do. If, despite the warnings of your compass, you find yourself in toxic relationships or discriminating situations, it is not a blow to your entire being. You can always reverse and fine-tune your compass so that it can continue to guide you lightly and gently toward the direction of joy.'

As Minna Salami says in her book, I too can say I am African and European. Paraphrasing her, I'd also say that I am mixed-race: a slow mix achieved over many centuries of trade from the Nile down to the Mediterranean, and from the Nile up to Nubian lands as far as ancient Abyssinia, centuries of mixing between sub-Saharans and Mediterraneans. I am Nilotic. I may have ancestors from Alexandria or from some corner of the southern Mediterranean, which is the north of the African continent. But I am also Catalan. With a Spanish passport. I've been Barcelonian. In Addis Ababa I feel very much at home. In Gondar and Bahir Dar too. Minna Salami says: 'My roots are embedded in the cultural expressions, sounds, tastes, and rhythms of life that we so easily take for granted until we are distanced from them.' And I could say the same about both my Catalan identity and my Ethiopian one. But where I most truly feel at home, where I created what Virginia Woolf called 'a room of one's own', is in Castellterçol. Amid the calm of the countryside, where the four seasons pass serenely through the trees. My refuge.

THE SOUNDS
OF MEMORY

In an article published on *Literary Hub* under the title 'The Wound of Multilingualism: On Surrendering the Languages of Home', the writer Sulaiman Addonia says: 'Amharic was a language of grief, violence, loss, unattained longing. I stepped out of it quickly.'

Talking to other young people of my age adopted from Ethiopia, I've found that many have fled their memories and allowed themselves to be embraced by their new reality. In the process, they have shied away from the confrontation inherent in opening and dusting off that imaginary box full of often unpleasant memories. I talk to them about the pain because I've lived it myself and have also experienced it through those people who have opened the door to their pain to me when they have found their biological families again, or because they haven't set foot in Ethiopia since leaving it as children. Some of us have stood by helplessly as, little by little, we have lost our mother tongue and along with it a whole code system which gave meaning to our lives.

⁊

In the summer of 2003, just before starting school in Barcelona for the first time, I continued to call Addis Ababa to speak to Kumbi. But there came a time when I stopped understanding him. I couldn't follow the conversation, couldn't find the words, and I stopped calling him. Or maybe it was that I stopped calling and because of that I couldn't understand him any longer. Addis Ababa was very far away from me. And I had so many things to do: learn two languages at once (Catalan and Spanish), understand new codes of behaviour, understand a new culture… Also learn to read and write, add and subtract, swim and ride a bike, discover foods I'd never tasted, and so many other new things. At seven years old I lost one of the few things I had then that was truly mine: my language.

⁊

In the context of international adoption there is much discussion of origins, about whether it's necessary to return or not, whether it's necessary to maintain contact with the biological family if the biological family is known. But what it means for a person to lose their mother tongue, their language of origin, isn't discussed enough. Luckily, a language can be learned and reclaimed, because it plays a key role in the formation of identity. Over a period of years – just a few – my Amharic was erased. Until, that is, my parents asked Abraham, a young man who in 2004 was in the process of opening the first Ethiopian restaurant in Barcelona, to come to our house once a week to teach me to read and write in Amharic, and go over the vocabulary I still knew: colours, numbers, the parts of the body... He called the restaurant he opened in Gràcia 'Abyssinia', the old name for Ethiopia. Later he opened another in the neighbourhood of Sants, naming it 'Addis Ababa', and the Gràcia one went to his sister Rahel. Those hours I spent with Abraham, hearing him speak in Amharic and being my enthusiastic teacher although he wasn't a proper teacher, gave me enough of a grounding to relearn my language on my own. With dedication and a huge amount of effort I began to sing again in Amharic, to understand what I was singing, and I regained, at least, the same linguistic level with which I'd left Ethiopia, bearing in mind that I spoke a very nomadic and not at all academic Amharic.

I never stopped listening to the songs of Aster Aweke and Gigi and so many other Ethiopian singers I'd heard in Dansha in particular. I remember the hours spent in Castellterçol that first summer in 2003, singing my whole repertoire of songs while Anna or Ricard recorded them on a cassette and video too.

How I liked hearing myself singing again, and how I laughed at myself when I watched the videos! I'd sing a lot, at all hours: painting with watercolours, which fascinated me, walking, looking out of the window, both at home and in the car. The *mezmur* songs made me slow down and helped me to 'digest' the enormous changes I was experiencing.

Constantly listening to Ethiopian songs and having mine recorded certainly helped me to retain a link to the words and sounds of Amharic, one that never really broke. In Dansha, we would listen to music on cassette and Yamrot would sing the Ethiopian classics; later, at the missionary centre in Addis Ababa, Lia, a young Ethiopian carer, would also play cassettes and we would sing together. Lia helped the missionaries any way she could, not least by giving attention to us children. She was then barely twenty years old and had been in the care of the missionaries since she was a little girl, ever since her mother had left her there to go and work in Sweden until she could collect her. And she did!

Realising at the age of ten, in 2006, that I couldn't understand anyone and that the people of my town, Wereta, didn't understand me any longer, affected me deeply. Not being able to express myself was upsetting. Perhaps it's one of the biggest traumas I've lived through: going back to Ethiopia, queueing in Addis Ababa airport to gain an entry visa and not understanding anything that the officials, who were simply asking where I had come from and where I was going, were saying to me. My eyes fill with tears every time I remember the shock, and how I felt then.

That sense of loss perhaps affected me a lot more than other friends of my age. I had no one in Ethiopia. When you have no family and no links to a place, the language is perhaps the only connection, the only possible link or vehicle to connect you with your roots. My relationship with Amharic has always been peculiar, given that I've sometimes rejected it.

It was during adolescence that I decided to relearn Amharic, teaching myself initially, then studying more formally through online courses. And I'm still going! It's been a very long process but I've persevered in my attempt to keep acquiring more knowledge, reading, listening to and speaking Amharic as often as I can (above all every time I've travelled to Ethiopia). In fact, if I have a clear goal in life it is to maintain the Amharic I've acquired and keep improving forever. Amharic is part of my primary identity; it's part of me.

Knowing Amharic is now my symbol of resistance against forgetting. I would argue that you cannot understand your origins without understanding the language. This applies to any place and language in the world.

ሕ

I met Tsion, Haile and all those who had arrived as adoptees later, when they were older than me (when they were already ten or eleven), in a meet-up organised by Haile, thanks to contact information given to him by AFNE so he could find us. We were teenagers, some fully grown, and out of that meeting came the group called Som Habesha (We Are Habesha), the idea being to bring Ethiopian culture to Ethiopian-Catalan families through our own initiatives. Then I realised that they were all Amhara. Having lived in Dansha and Humera, on the border between the regions of Amhara and Tigray, I'd been influenced a lot by Tigray, especially in my way of speaking and the lexicon I'd retained. When I would ask them the meaning of some word, thinking they were fluent in Amharic, they would often say: 'That doesn't mean anything.' It wasn't until years later that I discovered that those words that 'didn't mean anything' belonged to another language, Tigrinya, the language of Tigray.

The children who have left Ethiopia to be adopted around the world are Amhara, Oromo, Tigrayan, Sidama, Afar… But they'll all be seen simply as Ethiopian, without nuance. There will be no way for them to maintain their cultures and their languages. Despite the impressive digital progress that has revolutionised all sectors, today Google can only translate into Amharic and Oromo (given that it's similar to Somali). Most will lose their original language forever. And this makes me very sad.

Now I know that I grew up mixing Amharic and Tigrinya with Italian (which had taken root in the area after the occupation of Ethiopia by the Italian forces led by Mussolini from 1935 to 1939).

ሕ

In 2018, I went to the city of Mekelle, the capital of Tigray, with Tsion. She had found her biological brother, Biniam, on Facebook. They had exchanged photos for verification and in order to recognise each other. She was going back to see her paternal family in Tigray and I was accompanying her as her guest. I felt like an observer. Her maternal family in Addis Ababa and the neighbours who had cared for her as a little girl had welcomed me as one of them, and I was curious to see how my friend's paternal side would receive me. Tsion had a fascinating story and I learned a lot from her strength and courage in facing the past. In essence, she'd never broken with Ethiopia: she went back every year to spend a month with her aunt Mehiret and had never lost her Amharic. In part this was because she'd arrived in Catalonia at the age of eleven, educated and with much more consolidated language skills. Tsion would alternate her life in Barcelona with another in Addis Ababa, thereby connecting her two families and cultures. Once she landed at Bole international airport, she would become an urban Ethiopian, just like many of the diaspora who lived with one foot in Ethiopia and the other in the West. The fact that her link with Ethiopia was sustained by the existence of her biological family, and my link was purely voluntary, made me feel we formed a perfect duo. She and her Ethiopian family rooted me. With her natural elegance, Tsion is a born host. We have no aunt to bring us together, but in Barcelona Tsion imparts Ethiopian culture to us through her passion for food. She can spend hours preparing the *doro wat*, the misr and the *tibs* and seeking the most original mix of flours to achieve the *injera*'s authentic flavour: not too fermented and not too smooth. Why Tsion was adopted in Catalonia and didn't stay in Ethiopia and live with any of her relatives there is another story, solely hers.

During the three days we were in Mekelle I reconnected for the first time with the sounds of Tigrinya, a language which had been with me for a time in my childhood, a language I had claimed through the songs and jokes I'd heard on the streets of Dansha. In Mekelle, at twenty-two years old, I understood the importance of this information. During the Ashenda festival, three consecutive days of celebration of women, in a live music bar, I heard a poem recited in the Tigrayan language. It spoke of the origins, the struggle for identity and the emancipation of the population of Tigray. The melancholic tone of those voices made me realise that my project of research-ing my origins, which I'd begun before adolescence, wasn't limited to the state of Amhara. People rose to dance, and the oldest, who clearly were part of the diaspora and there on a visit, fluttered the Tigrayan flag in a show of patriotism and melancholy for the times of fighting. They were dancing in the middle of the restaurant, sticking birr notes on the foreheads of the dancers, and some of them flew through the air. The abundance of money and lack of control made me guess that many of them must have been young during the civil war in 1991 and gone abroad shortly afterwards.

In 2020, there were only six million people in Tigray, but they controlled a large part of Ethiopia. The Ashenda festival had become a tourist attraction which drew Ethiopians from the diaspora, and the Tigray flag provoked disparate feelings in the room. Some were whistling and commenting on the rapid political changes being introduced. Abiy Ahmed, an Oromo and member of the Oromo Democratic Party, would be the new prime minister, and at that time it meant a rebalancing of political power between the members of the coalition government of the EPRDF (Ethiopian People's Revolutionary

Democratic Front) and the TPLF (Tigray People's Liberation Front).

Like so many Ethiopians who condemn the ethnic federal system, I considered the division of Ethiopian politics along ethnic lines, in a country still with very little democratic political culture, to be a very dangerous solution. The preservation of multiple identities, cultures and languages lies in understanding that Ethiopians have always been a nomadic, heterogeneous society. Many of us feel trapped between multiple identities. I was born in the heart of the Amhara state and raised between two states: Amhara and Tigray. The resemblance between the women who filled the streets of Mekelle, dressed in traditional garments, and how I remembered Yamrot was so great that I noticed how a knot formed in my throat as they recited that poem. I only understood 'adey', the Tigrinya translation of 'haguere', a word which awakens all the feelings and links I forged as a little girl in Ethiopia. Adey and haguere mean the same thing: country. I left Mekelle having rediscovered a part of my identity that had marked my childhood, and with an even heavier backpack. I was more troubled than ever, because this time it would be more difficult to rebalance my identity. I would have to redefine my narrative, a task that seemed to be getting ever more complicated. As I grew up, it was becoming more difficult for me to resist forgetting.

And these moments of lucidity were like gusts of wind
that leave your muscles tense for days or even weeks.

What is clear to me is that Amharic will also
always be my refuge, my home. As long as I understand Amharic, I'll understand the little girl speaking
in the videos recorded in the documentary spirit by
Anna and Ricard during our first months together.
Amharic will always be my 'toolbox' for understanding the world where I was born.

FROM NAIROBI TO
ADDIS ABABA

Throughout summer 2019, after finishing my master's in Brussels, I'd made many applications to work in Ethiopia but hadn't had any luck, and it felt like I'd failed to throw the dice on an imaginary board. My first job brought me to Nairobi, the dynamic and cosmopolitan capital of Kenya, the most densely populated country in Africa, which shares a border and very good relations with Ethiopia. As a research intern in the International Crisis Group think tank, I focused on monitoring local media from their office in the Kilimani neighbourhood, to make a map of the magnitude and frequency of violence in Ethiopia, which was a victim of a vicious cycle of conflicts.

The Ethiopian community in Nairobi was one of the biggest I'd seen anywhere and it was well served. There was an Orthodox church in Kilimani, one of the city's most exclusive neighbourhoods. I didn't dare go in, even though I knew that that space was clearly the '*agora*' I was looking for. Although as a little girl I had had a strong faith, I cast off my religion

on arrival in Catalonia, like a snake shedding its
skin in summer. It was difficult to keep my acquired
doctrine in a house of atheists. Perhaps one of the
subjects I discussed most in Nairobi was religion.
I had long talks with Uber drivers about fate and luck,
about faith and fanaticism. They were frustrating
conversations that led nowhere, since neither the
taxi drivers nor I were ready to change our outlook
on life in a journey of twenty minutes maximum.
The *matatus*, minibuses decorated with graffiti and
retro photos inside and out, were mobile discos. If you
were lucky, you'd get out without being robbed. And
if there was no music, you had to listen to a religious
monologue from a learner reading the Bible, right in
the middle of a bus full of people, trying not to fall in
that constant shuddering of dusty, unpaved streets.

When I went to work in Nairobi, my friend
Elizabeth's family opened to me the doors of their
home 'at the foot of the Ngong Hills', not far from
the house where the Danish writer Karen Blixen had
lived. Elizabeth and I had met in Brussels, while she
was doing her master's in International Immigration,
and we shared classes discussing the intersection
between political conflict and immigration. After she
greeted me in Amharic with a '*Endemn nesh, yenne
konjo?*' we were never apart. She had learned very
good Amharic from living for a time in Addis Ababa
while working at the African Union. She taught

me many things about African culture and politics in general. Elizabeth's mother welcomed me like a fourteenth child: she already had nine daughters and four sons. All the names of her sons and daughters began with the letter E. And mine too. That was luck!

The family was a total matriarchy, and the running of it and the planning for the future of every member were part of an impressive system of leadership and training. The eldest siblings were well placed in very different fields: one worked at the African Union, another was a pilot, another worked at the British Consulate, one worked at the UN in finance, one worked in a hotel in Qatar... The eldest paid for the education of the youngest ones, who hadn't yet entered the world of work. The father was a quiet man and they were all part of the Catholic community in Ngong, helping families in need and organising Sunday Mass in the home of each member of the community. During my stay in their home, it was their turn to host a Sunday Mass. All the daughters living in Nairobi came to cook ugali, dengu, choma, chapatti and mandazi. We spent all morning in the kitchen, chatting about everything and nothing, dancing to the rhythm of songs in Swahili from Kenya and Tanzania, laughing loud and long, much more than a Mediterranean family would do.

Nairobi didn't hide its British colonial past, but at the same time it showed signs of being a developing city: it had a large and politically active middle class, an infrastructure which generated capital, and a deep feeling for nature and conservation. Many Kenyans hastened to tell me proudly that Nairobi had greater infrastructure than Addis Ababa because its middle class was much larger than in the Ethiopian capital. The Ngong road, which crosses the middle of the city, separating the neighbourhood of Karen (yes, named in honour of Karen Blixen and where her land was) from the Westlands and Westgate neighbourhoods, was being upgraded, broadened and resurfaced. These works made me think that if I came back to Nairobi after some time away it would be unrecognisable.

The city was divided by social class. You could lead a kind of European life, ignoring the misery of a large part of the population, with its slums and extremely poor areas within touching distance of the city. Seeing so many Europeans and Americans beginning their professional careers in the world of start-ups and humanitarian aid in an African country made a great impression on me. Those with an eye for trade had seen that there was a clear opportunity to bring technology to a society that needed ever more services. Some were trying to forge links between local and international industries, like cinema. For expats, the cost of living was very low and it was easy to save or travel around the region. Many foreign organisations had their headquarters close to Sudan,

Somalia and Ethiopia, zones declared unstable and unsafe, while they pulled strings from Nairobi.

Like many young expats, I ended up sharing a rented house in the Kilimani neighbourhood with five other young professionals, all European or American, who were also in Nairobi for six months or a year at most. They were all working in the research sector, whether in the field of agriculture, political conflict resolution (as in my case) or the economy. Little by little I was seeing that we expats formed a very endogamous community, very often reproducing our way of life from our places of origin but in a totally different context, the majority isolating themselves from reality and the local people. At weekends I'd go on hikes outside the city. Nairobi's hallmark was its landscape of green savannah, and the peaks of Kilimanjaro or Mount Kenya as seen from the terrace of the Kenyatta International Convention Centre. I went on the most recommended hikes (some more than once), such as the seven hills of Ngong, Karura natural park and Mount Longonot. The expats who had previously lived in our house had left some books behind. I'd arrived in the Kenyan capital with three books in my suitcase: *Decolonising the Mind* by Ngũgĩ wa Thiong'o, *The Emperor* by Ryszard Kapuściński, and *Capitalisme i democràcia 1756–1848: Com va començar aquest engany* (*Capitalism and Democracy 1756–1848: How This Fraud Began*) by Josep Fontana (this final one, in Catalan, is the one I would leave behind on departing). Later I'd go through the entire selection of books in the house until I discovered the Yaya Centre's magnificent bookshop.

In Nairobi I lost my independence, having been used to the general safety of Europe: everything I did had to be done with others. I depended on other people's availability to go to concerts, on hikes or even to the market. Being a woman and going around alone didn't work. My ability to go unnoticed drastically failed me. On the streets, men would stop me to start a conversation. I'd put my headphones in to go running and they'd stand in front of me. But what I found most incredible was having to urgently summon an Uber on my mobile and run out (as soon as the car was at the door) of a jazz session in Dagos Bar, or at Dagoretti Corner, where local artists were promoted, because a drunk man couldn't accept that I didn't want to talk to him or give him my number or hold his hand. I've never liked attention, and the fact that I wasn't respected was like a bucket of cold water. One more reminder of how much work remains to be done in terms of achieving equality between men and women.

፟ን

I'd been living in Nairobi for four months when I decided to travel to Addis Ababa from there: a short two-hour flight and a route with many daily flights. I landed in Addis Ababa mid-morning one Wednesday in early 2020. I'd never arrived during the dry season and by day. Tsion, who by chance was also in the city, came to meet me at the airport with her aunt Mehiret. During the journey to the city centre I couldn't stop thinking about the similarities between Addis Ababa and neighbouring Nairobi. I realised that the shock was much less than if I'd arrived from Barcelona. When I was little, every time I landed in Barcelona from Ethiopia I felt like I had come from a game of *The Sims*: everything impeccably neat and tidy, so well lit; I'd go so far as to say 'insultingly well lit'.

Shortly after having landed and eaten *alicha firfir* in a little restaurant nearby, I went to the home of Abraham and Tsigereda and their four children, my 'adoptive family' in Ethiopia. I needed to see them and for them to see me. I had met Abraham in 2012, during a family summer trip to Ethiopia, when my mother Anna was considering adapting into a film part of her novel *Rastres de sàndal* (*Traces of Sandalwood*), which had an Ethiopian as a main character, and was working on the screenplay. My parents ended up producing another part of the novel, which connected Mumbai, in India, to Barcelona, and gave it the same title as the book. Adapting the Ethiopian part was put on the back burner. Abraham, like many middle- and upper-class Ethiopians, had gained a grant to study abroad, in his case in the Netherlands, and later he'd returned to Ethiopia to found an audiovisual production company and the first film school in Addis Ababa. At eighteen, when I returned to Ethiopia on my own for the first time to complete my high school diploma research project about the development of the education system in Addis Ababa, Abraham and Tsigereda welcomed me into their home, located five minutes' walk from the University of Addis Ababa in the Sidist Kilo neighbourhood. And they became my family in Ethiopia. Their children were very clever. They'd been educated with an awareness of the social context in which they lived but also with ambitious minds, open to the international world. Heliana, who was then only twelve years old, was already quizzing me about universities and deliberating whether her academic future should be shaped by European or American values and standards of living.

Returning to Addis Ababa to have a meeting at the African Union and to visit Elizabeth's sister there – she was the representative of the Community of East African Countries at the Union – was a reality that neither Yamrot nor I at seven years old could ever have imagined. Lack of education deprives you of opportunities and reduces human experience. It is disheartening to think that in a country with such diplomatic power in the Horn of Africa, and in the

African continent as a whole, there are so many people deprived of being able to develop to their full potential. When women, and above all rural women, are kept from the role they could play in society, African governments are losing great talent. The same thing happens when we don't eradicate poverty or fight for universal, quality education: we limit ourselves as a society.

Given my life's journey, entering the African Union headquarters was like breaking down many walls and ceilings all at once – barriers that I'd never felt before me, but that were simply there because of my social background in Ethiopia. What was very strange for me was entering the African Union with a Spanish passport. Not going in there as an Ethiopian, but as a European who was going there to have a meeting. It was very clear to me that I was in there because I had a European passport, not because I was African.

The building of the African Union headquarters was built through international investment (German and Chinese above all) and it is very modern. There is so much inequality between the capital's infrastructure and that of the mostly rural remainder of the country. Finding myself inside that building, mindful of where I'd come from, of my origins, was overwhelming, difficult to process. Truly it was necessary to 'wear a hat for every situation', as Dalil had told me. In Addis Ababa I was seen as a European. And in any European city, I was seen, a priori, as an African. The layers of identity are therefore interesting, above all if you're ready to take it all philosophically and not get overexcited.

On that visit I became aware that Addis Ababa had numerous Ethio Rides, the local version of Uber known as 'the foreigner's ally' (the *farangi*'s ally), which had replaced many of the blue taxis in the city. As the Ethio Ride drivers took me from one meeting to another, I took the chance to practise my Amharic. Everyone noticed I was from elsewhere. I might be from Tigray or part of the Ethiopian diaspora returning to invest in the country's economy. With my broken, slightly strange accent (which means no one can ever tell where I come from) I'd ask the taxi drivers what they thought of the recent political changes and if the citizens' standard of living had changed under Abiy Ahmed's government. They answered that everything was fine in the capital, but they were worried about the situation and safety of their relatives living in the countryside. They told me: '*Teklai Ministeru tiru asab aleh*' ('The prime minister has good intentions'). But they were still waiting for the fruits of his democratic promise.

One day I ended up boarding a crowded and slightly dubious bus to go to the Institute for Peace and Security Studies (IPSS) at the University of

Addis Ababa. I had wanted to use an Ethio Ride taxi, but the internet wasn't working. The shutdown of the internet had become a regular occurrence; it was a tool for the government to control the entry and exit of information. A wide sector of society believed that the waves of violence that had taken place during Abiy Ahmed's term (the attempted coups, assassinations and revolts against the government) had been reduced thanks to the frequent disconnection of the phone lines and internet. When the market opened to the outside world, little by little the people who had launched online businesses started to see they were having to pay a very high price for the government's methods of establishing control over the country.

Another morning when I was in a hurry, the internet wasn't working and no buses were passing, so I got into a run-down old blue taxi without giving it much thought. In the middle of the roundabout to go from Sidist Kilo to Piazza, the rear doors flew open. Miraculously we didn't break the side mirrors or the windows of passing cars. I immediately tried to close one door, pulling it towards me as if I were trying to haul the sail of a boat against the wind, while the driver, still holding the wheel, closed the other.

In developing cities, change in transport management will hugely improve the standard of living of the entrepreneurial middle class, the true economic driver. In only a decade, Addis Ababa has changed very quickly. Luxury and misery coexist in an economic, social model of urbanism that is constantly growing. The elegant woman in a suit walking in high heels down a street under renovation lives side by side with the group of boys sitting under a tree in front of a fancy cosmetics shop sniffing glue from a plastic bottle.

ñ

I returned to Nairobi from Addis Ababa happy and at peace with my different identities. Then came the Covid-19 pandemic and my forced repatriation from Nairobi. 'Everyone to their healthcare service' was the motto of companies with expat workers.

The pandemic made it very clear that it respected neither economic nor political divisions. Everyone was fighting against a common enemy, a new and invisible enemy, with enormous consequences for the future of global relations. In fact, the pandemic also presented opportunities. For me, the most interesting thing was that it could be an opportunity to reverse the Western paternalism that, despite the end of political colonialism, had been maintained over time through a combination of new and old forms of domination and oppression in all fields: economic, cultural and social. Perhaps Europe would stop wanting to save Africa, which didn't need anyone to save it. But the systems of inequality survive anything, even a pandemic.

And a while later the bombing of Dansha would begin.

THE SCENT OF BURNT
EUCALYPTUS WOOD

After that long car journey from the missionaries' centre in Gondar with a driver, an unknown nun and a well-wrapped baby, I became used to daily life at the missionary centre in Addis Ababa. It was a much bigger place but had no garden. I didn't see it then, but now I know that there was an area for dying men, another for dying women, and yet another for very sick children. And a little building, the orphanage, where they kept all us boys and girls who were healthy (or seemed to be) well isolated, to avoid infection. The days in the centre run by the Calcutta missionaries in the middle of the city passed very slowly for me, while I found no answer to my questions. What had happened to Yamrot? Why had she died so quickly? And Mikaele? I didn't understand why nothing had happened to me and why I was there, so far away, with those women in the white saris, who ensured that the people working in the orphanage made us pasta and rice and gave us biscuits and bananas every day. In the centre they also stored donations from international humanitarian organisations and individuals. When I was following one of the nuns I'd see the piles of clothes they used to dress us, and the food parcels they received. I'd try to enjoy the moments when kind carers like Lia would have us sing the alphabet in English, all shouting at the top of our lungs.

One day they stood me in front of a brightly coloured mural and took my photo. Another day they took me to a doctor to get a blood sample. On yet another day a *farangi* appeared in the yard, accompanied by Sister Niharica, the director of the Addis Ababa centre. All the children except for me wanted to grab the sweets he had in his jacket pockets; I watched him from behind the wheelchair belonging to Aster, a girl my age who had polio, whom I helped move around and with whom I sometimes shared a bed. That *farangi*, who I'd later learn was called Santi Llensa, was the one who made the 'match' and decided that my new parents would be Ricard and Anna. A few weeks later the two came to meet me in that same yard. Everything was happening so fast, and I wasn't ready to leave so soon. I recognised them from a distance, because they were the *farangi* I'd seen in two photos they had sent me via another adoptive family, and I didn't like the look of them. The nuns were saying that 'my parents' would be coming to get me, but

I didn't understand. As I looked at the photos, I was thinking that what they were telling me was odd. Yamrot and Mikaele had died, and I had no intention of leaving with some strange white people. At that time, I was adapting quickly to places, and I'd forgotten about the photos of the two *farangi* until suddenly departure day came. They dressed me well, but in mismatched colours, as always, choosing the clothes from the pile of donations. Anna and Ricard documented it all. They'd arrived in Addis Ababa the day before, with four other families. With tears in my eyes I said goodbye to Aster, Lia and the missionaries, very scared and with no idea of what awaited me beyond the metallic door, which, like all Missionaries of Charity centres in the world, was painted turquoise.

⟪

Having been part of the 80 per cent of Ethiopian society that lives in the countryside, the vast majority of whom live on humanitarian aid from the government and international organisations, and the rest on the extreme poverty line, I constantly wonder if the statistics have changed. Over the last few years, there have been economic and political initiatives that will significantly improve the standard of living for those who most need it. The construction of GERD, the biggest dam in Africa, at the Blue Nile Falls (Tis Abay, to Ethiopians) is an example.

On 8 July 2021, after ten years of conflict between Egypt, Ethiopia and Sudan about the construction of GERD, the dispute reached the table of the UN Security Council. The representatives of the three countries were unable to reach a consensus about key aspects of the agreement, such as the management of the dam. The conflict had acquired an international dimension when in July 2020 Ethiopia began the first phase of filling the dam with water to test the working of the turbines in the rainy season without having finalised the agreement. The main international players, especially the United States, weighed in on the argument of the discussions. Ethiopia stuck firmly to its plan despite threats of a military attack and the international pressure exerted at the negotiations in Washington and Kinshasa. The matter reached the UN Security Council because Egypt saw the mega-project as a threat both to their principal source of drinking water and to their agriculture, and because the dam reversed the water hegemony Egypt had enjoyed on the continent thanks to colonial pacts that Ethiopia didn't recognise. The dam was the promise of a more dignified, prosperous future and of self-sufficiency. For the first time with a project of such magnitude, Ethiopians of all ideologies and social classes had contributed to the construction with money from their own pockets. Ethiopians believed that this dam would not only be a source of development for their country, but would also benefit neighbouring countries. But, in the context of the challenges generated by climate change, the project had become politicised and, as often happens in such situations, those who would be most affected were forgotten.

I wonder what the girl on the bus would say, the one who left Dansha sitting beside the window with her sick mother and little brother, if she had stayed in Ethiopia, a country full of contradictions, that aspired to develop itself politically, economically and socially against the odds. What would she say if the possibility of living a dignified life was limited by colonial agreements that prioritised the drums of war rather than peaceful dialogue?

The fight to obtain the same opportunities for all and reduce violence is perhaps one of the most important for young people of my generation, in Ethiopia and around the world: to break the cycles of violence and to cultivate the seeds of prosperity. In 2021 only 20 per cent of Ethiopia's villages had electricity, and sixty-five million people lived without it. This meant thousands of women and girls having to walk many kilometres every day to gather wood and carry it home tied to their backs to be able to cook and heat water. It meant having fewer hours of light and inadequate conditions for daily activities such as study. It meant not paving roads or building new ones to connect the rural world to the urban world. The dam megaproject was an ambitious project to make use of the country's under-exploited resources to generate wealth and therefore opportunities.

Ethiopia was in the process of redefining itself, and in this process the role of the rural and urban Ethiopian woman was key. As the president of Ethiopia, Sahle-Work Zewde, has said on various occasions: 'A window of opportunity has opened; it is our responsibility to make the most of it.'

The first stage of my life was shaped by Yamrot's death, which uprooted me from Ethiopia – 'uprooted' in every sense of the word – and saw me reconstructing my identity in Catalonia. Refusing to forget. Now I'm beginning my adult life equipped with all the tools and opportunities that have been offered to me and that I've found. And I feel I can't begin it without speaking of Yamrot, who died at the age I am now, at twenty-five, in Gondar. A place that has been a magnet since I left it. Even though I've been lucky enough to go back whenever I wanted, understanding the socio-economic and political situation in Ethiopia has truly been my way of returning to my origins. Nostalgia for the past is a well-known feeling for those who, like me, have been uprooted for whatever reason. Nostalgia is the force that makes us return time and again to our roots to understand what made us leave. And also to change what prevented us from exploiting our potential. Perhaps one of my greatest discoveries has been realising that the return to one's origins isn't only physical: knowledge can also shorten distance and time. I devote myself to better understanding Ethiopia's situation. Out of necessity. To redefine who I am and where I want to go.

If I close my eyes now, wherever I am, I can smell the same scent of burnt eucalyptus wood as the girl on the bus. The day this scent is a distant memory for other Ethiopian girls too will be the day that we've moved forward. It will mean that all rural parts of Ethiopia have access to electricity. It will mean that this weight on rural girls and women to keep going for their families, their community and therefore their country, by carrying wood and cans of water on their backs from one village to another, has grown lighter. Lightness will help us move forward.

Author's Note

I finished writing this book in November 2021, when
the armed conflict in northern Ethiopia was still
active.

Glossary

Adey abeba   Yellow wildflowers that grow in Ethiopian fields after the rainy season. Also known as Meskel flowers.

Alicha firfir   Dish from Ethiopian cuisine based on stewed vegetables.

Amhara   Relating to the Amhara region in northern Ethiopia, where Amharic is spoken.

Arake   Alcoholic beverage made from the distillation of cereals.

Aranguadi   The colour green.

Ashenda   Known as the 'women's festival', it is especially celebrated in Tigray and northern Ethiopia. It began as a religious festival but has evolved into a cultural festival where singing and dancing predominate.

Bajaj   Small three-wheeled vehicle that serves as public transport, very similar to the rickshaws in India.

Berbere   A blend of powdered aromatic roasted spices that is used in Ethiopian cuisine.

	Often used to cook stews with meat or red lentils.
Birr	Ethiopian currency.
Bitcha	The colour yellow.
Bunna	Coffee.
Bunna bet	Cafeteria, a place where coffee is served (and sometimes food too).
Dabo	Bread made from cornflour, usually round and very thick.
Doro wat	Chicken fried with tomato, onion and spices.
Enkulal firfir	Egg scrambled with onion.
Enkutatash	The first day of the month of Meskerem in the Ethiopian calendar (11 September in the Gregorian calendar), which marks the start of the Ethiopian new year.
Falasha	Jews of Ethiopia.
Farangi	Foreigner.
Fasika	Orthodox Ethiopian Easter.
Genfo	A thick porridge made from wheat flour served with niter kibbeh (clarified Ethiopian butter) and *berbere*.
Gojo	Little house made of adobe with a roof formed of tree branches.
Injera	The basis of Ethiopian cuisine and the basis of all meals. It consists of a kind of crepe made from fermented teff (local cereal) flour, which accompanies stews such as *doro wat*, misr wat (thick puréed lentils), etc.

Kay	The colour red.
Kebele	The smallest local entity of administration, which might be equivalent to a neighbourhood or urban zone. The next level up is the *woreda*.
Kemis	Also known as *habesha kemis*, this is the long traditional dress of Ethiopian women, worn at all festivals. It is made from white cotton, and its borders are embroidered in different colours.
Kolo	A mix of roasted cereals and chickpeas that people often carry as a snack.
Mastica	Chewing gum.
Mezmur	A form of religious song practised by the Ethiopian Orthodox Church.
Misr	Lentils.
Netela	White cotton dress with a coloured border on the outside that Ethiopian women use to cover themselves, especially when entering an Orthodox Christian church. Some men also wear them as outer garments.
Nikisat	Traditional Ethiopian tattoo.
Oromo	Relating to the Oromia region of Ethiopia, which has its own language (Oromo) and a flourishing culture.
Serratenya	Maid.
Shiro	Chickpea sauce.
Suk	Market.

Tibs   Typical dish of diced meat and spicy sauce.

Warka   Tree native to Ethiopia, at risk of extinction. There are some that are more than a hundred years old, mostly in the north of the country.

Acknowledgements

This story exists thanks to so many hours of conversation with adopted people and those from the Ethiopian diaspora. But, most of all, it exists thanks to my parents, Ricard Domingo and Anna Soler-Pont, who have always left novels by Ethiopian authors or about Ethiopia in the piles of books around the house, which I have devoured one after the other. I also thank them for passing on the value of memory and an interest in history and origins.

I am very grateful for the comments of the readers of the first draft of the manuscript: Eulàlia Comas Lamarca, Izaskun Arretxe and Laura Quero. And also for the observations of Haile Fàbrega.

My thanks to the entire Pontas literary agency team for their support.

Having a publisher like Ernest Folch for my original Catalan text has been a luxury, and I appreciate the dedication of the entire Navona publishing team. Having a publisher like Susie Nicklin, with her passion, has been another gift. Many thanks to the entire team at The Indigo Press. And my thanks to Laura McGloughlin for the first draft of the English translation.

Thank you to all the people who are mentioned, and to those who have accompanied me on my journey to these pages.

Transforming a manuscript into the book you hold in your hands is a group project.

Ennatu would like to thank everyone who helped to publish *Burnt Eucalyptus Wood*.

The Indigo Press Team

Susie Nicklin
Phoebe Barker
Honor Scott

Jacket Design

Luke Bird

Publicity

Claire Maxwell

Foreign & Audiovisual Rights

Pontas Agency

Editorial Production

Tetragon
Robina Pelham Burn
Sarah Terry

THE
INDIGO
PRESS

The Indigo Press is an independent publisher of contemporary fiction and non-fiction, based in London. Guided by a spirit of internationalism, feminism and social justice, we publish books to make readers see the world afresh, question their behaviour and beliefs, and imagine a better future.

Browse our books and sign up to our newsletter for special offers and discounts:

theindigopress.com

The Indigo Press app brings our books and exclusive bonus content to readers around the world. Available now on iOS, Android, and your web browser.

Follow *The Indigo Press* on social media for the latest news, events and more:

🐦 @PressIndigoThe
📷 @TheIndigoPress
📘 @TheIndigoPress
▶️ The Indigo Press
🎵 @theindigopress